TRACKING
FREEDOM

Books by Ken Eagle Feather

Traveling with Power
The Exploration and Development of Perception

A Toltec Path
A User's Guide to the Teachings of don Juan Matus,
Carlos Castaneda, and other Toltec Seers

Tracking Freedom
A Guide for Personal Evolution

TRACKING

TRACKING FREEDOM

A Guide for Personal Evolution

KEN EAGLE FEATHER

HAMPTON ROADS PUBLISHING COMPANY, INC.

FREEDOM

Cover design by Marjoram Productions
Cover art by Rosemarie Crocker
Text illustrations by David Brown

For information write:
Hampton Roads Publishing Company, Inc.
134 Burgess Lane
Charlottesville, VA 22902
Or call: (804)296-2772
FAX: (804)296-5096
e-mail: hrpc@hrpub.com
Web site: http://www.hrpub.com

If you are unable to order this book from your local
bookseller, you may order directly from the publisher.
Quantity discounts for organizations are available.
Call 1-800-766-8009, toll-free.

Library of Congress Catalog Card Number: 98-71581

ISBN 1-57174-093-7

10 9 8 7 6 5 4 3 2 1

Printed on acid-free paper in Canada

DEDICATED
TO
PURE UNDERSTANDING,
WHICH IS THE FIRM UNDERSTANDING
THAT NOTHING IS EVER UNDERSTOOD.

ACKNOWLEDGEMENTS

For their impeccable editorial considerations—not to mention their lasting friendship—a tip of the hat goes to Michele Flamingo, Greg Helmers, and Dan Questenberry.

Special thanks to Bob Friedman, Kathy Grotz, and Gail Wiley . . .

. . . all of whom prove that a good editor is a writer's best friend.

"In the beginner's mind there are many possibilities, but in the expert's there are few."

—Shunryu Suzuki
from *Zen Mind, Beginner's Mind*

"The things that people do cannot under any conditions be more important than the world. And thus a warrior treats the world as an endless mystery and what people do as endless folly."

—don Juan Matus
from Carlos Castaneda's *A Separate Reality*

CONTENTS

1

WHAT'S UP?

I first passed don Juan Matus on a main drag in Tucson while hurriedly walking to class at the local university. I first talked with him in the parking lot of a small market on the outskirts of Tucson. I first *saw* him while we were in a rather nondescript section of the same city. And the last time I was physically with him was near the same market where I first engaged him face-to-face.

These encounters illustrate a blueprint—an omen, if you will—of our association. In the hubbub of the city, I simply noted his presence and passed him as I was too caught up in the movement of my life—even though I had moved to Tucson with the intent of meeting a Toltec seer, an honest-to-goodness wizard. A few days later, a face-to-face meeting occurred on the outskirts of city life, very appropriate in that Toltec knowledge currently exists on the outskirts of contemporary civilization. Years later, I *saw* him as pure energy in exquisite balance with the energy of the world, and did so in a setting that de-emphasized the material world. Then we came full circle to wrap up things just about where we had begun.

Don Juan, as you may know, is the central figure in the best-selling books of Carlos Castaneda. Pointing the way into a magical and mystical avenue of human experience, their association has lighted up the imagination of people the world over. As an anthropology student, Castaneda was researching psychotropic (often referred to as hallucinogenic) plants used by Native Americans. This pursuit led him to don Juan, who turned out to be an extremely adept sorcerer, shaman, seer, magician, Toltec—whatever label serves—who guided Castaneda into an awareness of the world and ourselves as energy.

My encounters with don Juan turned my world upside down, to where I eventually could tell what was right side up. Before our meeting my life had lost all meaning. Languishing in doubt, I didn't know where I was, or where I should go. This emotional malaise was only one problem. Due to internal bleeding, on more than one occasion I vomited blood and had to be hospitalized. In short, I was having a wretched life and was on a fast track to the grave. Practicing the exercises in Castaneda's books brought the only healing I could find. Indeed, over the years don Juan's Toltec world has given me physical, emotional, mental, and spiritual renewal. His teachings literally saved my life as they opened the avenue into a new relationship with the world.

As a means to bring this renewal about, don Juan gave me a learning task. He said I should write two books about Castaneda's books, to shed light on them. Accomplishing this naturally required that I earnestly learn what was in them. Completing this task took eighteen years to the month. For sixteen of those years, I worked on the task without ever missing a day. The last two were for finishing touches. The first of these books, *Traveling With Power*, gives an account of how I met don Juan, as well as basic procedures to enter the Toltec world. The second book, *A Toltec Path*, provides what I consider to be the overall structure of don Juan's teachings. In turn, *Tracking Freedom* represents how to enact the structure, how to make it work for you for forever and a day. It also represents a personal consolidation of the task, and sets the stage for a new direction. Accordingly, while this book will be my last detailed analysis of don Juan's teachings as related to Castaneda's books, the task set into motion a love for writing that may spawn several more works of different natures. In short, the task has effectively restored meaning in my life.

Scrutinizing Castaneda's books, a complete philosophical system emerges. They contain a sophisticated worldview to focus energy, as well as discipline and techniques to harness energy. As a metaphysical philosophy, the Toltec Way deals with the nature of reality, including how reality is perceived, formulated, and experienced. Furthermore, it is not only a system of thought, it is a philosophy of action, of behavior.

A good metaphysical philosophy always has two elements. First, it has within it the seeds of its own destruction, or its own transcendence, however you care to look at it. Consistent with don Juan's teaching, a system is a tool to enhance personal development. It's not something to be followed blindly. This is partly why he shuns being anyone's master, and pokes fun at those who consider themselves "official sorcerers in residence" (*Dreaming,* 2).[1] It is also why he accents developing raw potential over living by the dictums of a philosophy. Second, a viable system is non-exclusive. That is, if you're a practicing Toltec, Hindu, Christian, or whatever, and someone from another faith or discipline offers a tool that works well for you, you don't arbitrarily ignore it because it's not *your* philosophy. Accordingly, at times I relate the work of The Monroe Institute (TMI) to Toltec perspectives.[2]

I became involved with TMI in 1983, when I traded writing a magazine article for participation in one of their week-long seminars, a "Gateway Voyage." The results were simply phenomenal, as their Hemi-Sync™ technology took my fellow participants and me into lands of perception far beyond the ordinary. I've since taken three other seminars, and had twenty-two individual sessions in their laboratory. *Traveling With Power* offers an overview of the Institute, its technology and programs, as well as my experiences during many of these adventures.

In a nutshell, by listening to specific audio signals, Hemi-Sync™ supports balancing the electrical activity between the right and left hemispheres of the brain. Since both halves of the brain are communicating—indeed, working in harmony—you automatically access perceptions that had been latent. Thus, you bring to life more of your potential. This balance within self also elevates perception into heightened awareness.

Aware that language biases perception, TMI aims for neutral terms to describe the effects of Hemi-Sync™. Hence, *focus level* simply means being attentive to, or focused within, a particular aspect of consciousness. Focus 10, for example, is "mind awake/body asleep." In Focus 10, people uniformly report being awake within awareness not associated with their physical bodies. Focus 21, for another example, deals with "alternate energy systems." Travel to worlds removed from this physical Earth is often reported.

Because the Institute has labeled these experiences, and can consistently produce them through its technology, the stage is set for a doctrine to emerge. People with shared experiences tend to seek common ground. Beliefs and dogma then emerge. Fortunately, people will also find disagreements. In so doing, even if a disagreement is a pain in the butt, it prevents mindless adherence to a belief. One argument against Hemi-Sync™, for instance, is that during a seminar a group-mind effect produces a self-fulfilling prophecy whereby people experience just what they think they are supposed to experience. This is a great perspective to balance the intensity of the programs. At the same time, TMI's strength is that it avoids establishing beliefs whenever possible. Yet some kind of structure is necessary to enable communication. Optimally, knowledge of how language and doctrine trap perception rescues the quest for freedom by allowing participants to use the tools deliberately, not be used by them. In fact, it's commonplace for people to innovate and tailor their experiences during a seminar. Once shifts among focus levels are experienced, it's easy to intend shifts outside the scope of the exercises. You may then explore to suit yourself. Therefore, while seminar participants learn to communicate about having shared specific regions of awareness, they also have unique experiences.

Toltecs also use technology, although it's more low-tech; *natural* might even be a better word. A variety of meditative practices combined with the strenuous pursuits of *losing self-importance* and the *gait of power* (a manner of running that may be used any time of the day or night, in any terrain), for example, serve to awaken perception. Since a highly refined worldview is coupled with the technology, a broad-based philosophy emerges. This at once creates strength and weakness. Its strength is that you can account for anything in your world. You can explain anything that happens to you, even when it occurs while engaging another philosophy. A change in focus levels, for example, could be interpreted from a Toltec perspective as a shift in *cohesion*. Cohesion pertains to the pattern of energy in a personal energy field, and is discussed in the next chapter. One weakness is that you may lose yourself within this accountability. You'll forever be true to the system, to those beliefs, and never be true to an even greater potential locked within you. The value of combining systems, such as a metaphysical system and Hemi-Sync, is that you stand a better chance of staying open and thus leverage your awareness out of any ruts.

Following a specific path is highly advantageous. There is too much to handle, to explore, and to learn, to be able to travel far and wide without the strong support and the road markers offered by a philosophy. For any lifestyle to be effective, you must immerse yourself within it. Consistent behavior delivers results. A well-honed system slices through awareness and allows you to awaken the power to make the journey. Plus, a workable system also teaches you how to evolve beyond it—a double-edged sword.

Throughout this book, I repeatedly present this notion of simultaneously using, and getting trapped by, a system because I *see* a system not only as a force for liberation, but also as the single, most stultifying influence in the lives of those who engage a spiritual quest. To manage these influences effectively, I think they need to be understood from a variety of angles.

A philosophy acts as a guidance system. Naturally it guides you to its own destination, stopping at places within it. The Toltec Way, for instance, has a goal of freedom, of entering dimensions far removed from normal human considerations, of becoming pure energetic awareness. In the quest for this goal, Toltecs make pit stops in inorganic worlds, talk with elemental nature spirits, and learn personal energy management. Thus, by freely entering alternate realities, Toltecs find that the fantasies that people play with are often real events. Above all else, though, is a Toltec's unrelenting quest to lose self-importance, to break all boundaries restricting perception. Most of these boundaries, as we'll explore, define how we describe and interpret our world.

The Toltec world is a world of energy. Accordingly, Toltecs describe the world in the terms of energy fields, and people in terms of their energy bodies. As a philosophy, the Toltec study of the world as energy is also known as *nagualism*. Nagualism is an ancient body of knowledge rooted in central Mexico, and is an underpinning of many Mayan and Toltec practices. In the last thirty years, this knowledge has been brought to light and popularized by Castaneda acting in the role of an anthropologist. Don

Juan also uses the term *nagual* to refer to a luminous energy field, as well as to the energy body. The term also describes people, such as don Juan and Castaneda, who have a particular configuration in their personal energy fields. Naguals are *seen* as having a double energy body. This enhancement of energy makes them natural leaders of Toltecs (*Dreaming*, 10).

Don Juan has also referred to the Toltec world as *sorcery*, and its practitioners as *sorcerers*. While these terms are intriguing, they may be inadequate to carry the full meaning of what Toltec teachings offer. As we'll discover, Toltec philosophy has grown out of its own dark age and easily accepts the light of day, revealing the potential for it to be a major force in understanding the human condition, thereby understanding human evolution.

To develop the awareness of the world as energy, Toltecs use strategies and tactics. An example of strategy is outlining a goal and then engaging several energy maneuvers to get there. If your goal is to awaken your energy body (a preliminary of heading for freedom), you can use the broad-based energetic maneuvers of *tracking* and *dreaming*. These terms reflect different types of energy, as well as different ways of handling energy. Tracking is calculating, stable, growth-through-steps, and logical. Don Juan also refers to this energy as *stalking*.[3] Dreaming, on the other hand, is wide-open expansion, anything goes, irrational as you can make it, and simply mind-boggling. By using both, then balancing both, you've taken a significant step toward managing your resources.

Developing *body knowledge* is another key ingredient of strategy. This means learning to use the body's complete resources rather than relying solely on the intellect. Toltec knowledge deems that the body as a whole is attuned to infinite order, and the intellect to a very narrow margin of order. Mentally handling something is not the same as *knowing* it. An idea is not the thing itself. Much of the struggle to learn Toltec ways, therefore, involves letting go of the intellect in order to allow the body to rule.

Tactics, then, are the more immediate maneuvers, the bits and pieces that build strategic success. One tactic is acknowledging *personal responsibility* for each and every thought and action. You must seize the reins of your life; otherwise, you'll get squashed from the influence of the new energy fields you'll be tapping. This is not a dire situation. There is no bogeyman lurking. The path just requires responsible, sober behavior. Another tactic is *altering routines*, or deliberately changing your daily habits. This includes your habits for perceiving reality.

Harnessing strategies and tactics brings to life the *cornerstones of perception*, the vehicles that permit the direct perception of energy. Cornerstones are also components of the energy body; thus, they are part of body knowledge. *Seeing*, for instance, is any type of direct perception. You might intuitively feel you're in the midst of nature spirits, kinesthetically sense an answer to a puzzling question, or have a vision of your path in life. What distinguishes *seeing* from looking at something is that *seeing* deals directly with the energy that people, places, and things are made up of. Therefore, *seeing* not only allows you to develop and employ strategy, it eventually gives you the option of leaving the system—for you can also *see* what the philosophy is, and how and why it works.

Toltecs, then, are metaphysicists as they deal with worlds within worlds and the energies that create and sustain them. They are metaphysicians in that they seek to restore balance in their lives. They seek to produce healing. The gist of it is that Toltecs are explorers, scouts, and adventurers looking to claim their beingness in all of its totality. Don Juan, for instance, has such awareness of his natural condition that he can literally turn his physical body into pure energy just as another person might feel comfortable flying an airplane. One hallmark of this lifestyle is arriving at the discipline of a *ranger*, which don Juan refers to as a *warrior*. A ranger is one who has learned the essentials of the path and is aiming to evolve to yet another level.

In the pursuit of freedom, Toltecs weave their knowledge throughout their daily lives. It's not a matter of working 9 to 5, then donning a cape and becoming a marauding Toltec. A Toltec's evolution forms from the serious (and often fun-filled) study and enactment of a lifestyle that has grown with each successive Toltec generation over the course of thousands of years. There was a time when Toltec practices centered on the coarse manipulation of people. Perhaps this could be considered the age of sorcery, as the term *sorcery* carries that flavor. But don Juan was one of many who broke those shackles, and in the process formed a new cycle of thought and action. The new cycle hinges on freedom, for one and all. Now, with Castaneda's writings providing a stable reference, and mainstream societies itching to get a taste of Toltec and like-minded teachings, I think we are at the dawn of yet another cycle of Toltec endeavors.

One recent Christmas Eve, for example, I was watching a television broadcast that concerned healing through prayer. Another station carried a show on miracles. If these shows had been on a number of years ago, they would have been seen by the majority of viewers as tabloid journalism—if they were broadcast at all. Times are changing; a new stage of our evolution may be taking hold. So please keep this in mind as you consider the options presented here. While some of these may seem outlandish, in the coming years they may gain a wider foothold.

To know the fullness of the Toltec path, it is necessary to understand don Juan's perspective that most people following the path think they are performing magic, engaging in sorcery, or pursuing some similar undertaking (*Silence*, 10–11). He contends, rather, that these people are cultivating advanced human potential, evolving through levels of imagination, if not becoming imagination itself: the supernatural becoming natural. This strikes a deep chord. Because what counts is the unbridled expansion of awareness, not regimentation. Therefore, the challenge of this book is for me to remain true to the highest of Toltec teachings to the best of my ability. Accordingly, this is the way I *see* it. In no way does it supersede Castaneda's work. Indeed, to date his books—more than any other Toltec-related books—carry the weight of don Juan's teachings.

You'll find a little overlap of material in this book with my previous work. For example, I've again outlined many tracking and dreaming skills, as well as elements of the energy body. But to invigorate these perspectives, I present new insights and how-to exercises. In addition, the overall thrust of this book is different. *Traveling With Power*, for example, offers an introduction to the Toltec world, an overview of TMI, and many basic step-by-step exercises for tracking and dreaming. *A Toltec Path*, in turn, provides a one-volume reference for Toltec history, philosophy, and procedures as presented in the books of Castaneda. The main theme here is evolution: the dynamics of it, and the how to do it. In other words, where this path takes you, and what may happen along the way.

You don't have to be on a metaphysical path to know that what people tell you is not always so. As don Juan says, we have learned to live our lives incorrectly to perfection. Therefore, Toltecs begin with the assumption that they are out of balance and then work diligently to restore it (*Tales*, 34). It's easy to see how humans around the globe are out of balance. We continue to lay waste to our planet, to battle others of our species, and to teach our children how to handle money but not how to build a meaningful life. We are estranged from our essential nature of expansive potential, the energy of which leads to freedom. If what we held true was truly in balance, we would not face these kinds of difficulties. The quest for evolutionary transformation, then, is the quest for freedom. And for this, balance within self, with others, and with the world at large is required. Since it is helpful to know the guiding lights of your quest before embarking, it is my hope that I will provide you yet a bit more light.

At times, you'll view a system as a bunch of psychobabble. Well, in a way this is true. However, unless you're gifted, you need a system to elevate you to an enhanced relationship with the world. Then, when you have achieved a most remarkable balance, you can leave the system behind. This book, therefore, is also a concise guide for people trying to figure out what spiritual disciplines are, how they help, and how they can hold you back. In this light, *Tracking Freedom* uses modern Toltec philosophy as a sounding board to present the dynamics of metaphysical systems. It is my most fervent wish that I have done so in a manner that enables practically anyone to use this book to embark toward freedom's gate.

PART I

THE
ENERGY
OF
EVOLUTION

2

THE WORLD AS ENERGY

We typically view the world as made up of material, solid objects. Toltecs offer another option.

"Everything is energy," says don Juan. "The whole universe is energy." According to don Juan, *seeing* the world as energy is a matter of direct perception, not the predator's stance of objectively classifying the environment as is done for obtaining food and enhancing survival. Don Juan continues by saying that perceiving the world as external objects hinges on the agreements we collectively make about the world, agreements that have been handed down for centuries without us taking the time to challenge them. As a result, we have produced a world based on a collection of assumptions *about* reality. In other words, we have inherited a description of reality so powerful that we have validated it time and time again without ever having learned to step beyond it (*Dreaming*, 3-4).

By viewing the world as material, we have produced a world of glimmering shadows, of resting our perception on the surface of reality. Even then, we have built an amazing world. But think of the power that waits beyond the surface. Nonordinary perception such as *seeing*, as an example of this power, is considered by most Toltecs as an enhancement of our abilities. It cuts through the glimmering and deals directly with what is being perceived. Now, the notion—including the actual perception—of the world as energy is also a description of reality. It is generated by social agreements backed up by generations of people perceiving the world as such. Therefore, not to challenge the results of this advanced mode of perception places us in the same boat don Juan tries to roll us out of, as when he talks about social agreements being handed down without examining them.

Accordingly, I *see* that using the term *energy* is a practical way to describe a dynamic that occurs within awareness itself. What is actually there, or what actually occurs, is something so abstract it will remain elusive for eternity. For to render it sensible and concrete at any turn of the road removes perception from the abstract, from evolutionary potential, from *pure understanding*. As don Juan says, modern Toltecs strive to "steer away from concreteness toward the abstract" (*Dreaming,* 2). Pure understanding, then, never exceeds having a sense of the things about you, never calcifies perception, yet always transforms the way you relate to the world.

Indeed, a Toltec quest for the abstract is the quest for freedom, which is the ability to perceive all that's humanly possible. This journey also removes Toltecs from the social underpinnings that generate our ordinary reality. Since modern Toltecs do not focus on material gain or social status, they don't set up shop as having *the* official, or *the* authentic, Toltec perspective (*Dreaming,* 2). They're too much into freedom to do so—and this includes allowing others to have theirs. Anyway, back to viewing the world as energy.

Energy is often measured as vibration, or frequency. For instance, the AM and FM bands on your radio are regions of energy. Each region has its own nature; the FM band consists of higher vibrations than does the AM band.

This is not necessarily good or bad. FM tends to have clearer reception, but generally does not travel the distance that AM frequencies do. The use of one or the other depends on what your goal is.

Vibrations of energy—natural *emanations*—affect us in many ways. We sense heat and cold, for example. In the more rarified forms of energy, we can *feel* it and *see* it. In its various material forms, we can touch and smell it, taste and hear it. If it is dense enough, we can sit on it. Or we can mold it and fly through the air in it, as with airplanes. Energy perceived and handled as though it were solid has built magnificent civilizations, but it has also built skyscrapers that block our view of the natural world. Changing our relation to the world—in this case, agreeing that the world is comprised of pure energy from which material objects are formed—lets us sail over the skyscrapers that block imagination.

Actually, they don't block anything. Skyscrapers also originate from our imagination. The point is that by emphasizing a three-dimensional, subject-object world we tend to block out a world where our bodies are one and the same with the world. This world of oneness is the world of energy. Typically, you can't *see* it until you recognize it. Odds are, you won't recognize it until you open up to it.

Types of Energy

One of the neat things about Toltec theory is that by relating to the world as energy, it bridges its philosophy with that of others. Science, especially physics, for instance, also views the world as energy. This bridge enables you to cross over in each direction, and thereby loosen the grip of either world. Having common features allows Toltec theory to be applied to the general world. Using it to awaken the energy body, for example, allows you to experience yourself as energy without having to subscribe to the Toltec world. For up-and-coming Toltecs, this also sets the stage to grow beyond the system. Since "energy" speaks to a universal human condition, you can use a Toltec-built bridge to cross over into freedom.

As with any theory, it's possible to make an extensive inventory of various types of energy and their effects. If we hold that the world is energy, then each person, place, and thing in the world is energy. Each group of items, such as humans, trees, or clouds, has its own dynamics. Then there is another set of dynamics for how these groups interact. For our purposes, let's look at several forms of energy and relate them to the work at hand. The more you recognize the influences of your environment and what is at work within you, the more you're aware of yourself, your circumstances, and your evolution.

Potential. This is energy that lies in store, holds the possibilities, and waits to be actualized.

Realized. This is energy that is expressed, that blossoms out of potential into manifestation. Realized energy is taking your potential and grooming it into life. If you recognize your own artistic potential, for instance, you can set about the task of actualizing it through study and practice. Humans, for another example, have magical potentials for sophisticated dreaming. Toltecs aim to realize this potential.

Eagle. Don Juan refers to the Eagle as the source of creation. The Eagle's energy therefore contains and commands all aspects of creation. The Eagle also contains the potential of all creation. Through its emanations, it contains the realization of that potential (*Fire*, 51).

Emanations. The specific vibrations or frequencies generated by the Eagle are emanations (*Fire*, 53). Each aspect of creation has its own emanation, or band of energy, if you will. Thus, there is an emanation for humans, for extraterrestrials, for plants, and for trees, just to name a few. Emanations are the Eagle realizing aspects of itself.

During a TMI program, I *saw* the Eagle as a dark cloud of void. When I intended to go past the focus level I was in, I *saw* its emanations as lines of softly luminous energy projecting out of the cloud. During the same program I also *saw* the Eagle as an ever-expanding, concentrated mass of energy containing infinite potential. After the program I continued having visions of the Eagle and its emanations. I even had several while writing this part of the book. As I was focusing on writing about the Eagle, *seeing* it occurred. Indeed, a maxim of TMI is that focused consciousness holds the solutions to all of our problems. Hence, focusing on the topic "Eagle" produced more awareness of it, more *seeing* it.

Spirit. In many metaphysical philosophies, Spirit is considered the most powerful form of energy. It is often considered the source of All That Is. However, in philosophies where the "most-high" position is given to God, then Spirit is considered the direct agent of God, the force through which God influences creation. From a Toltec perspective, Spirit is the mysterious agent of the Eagle.

Line. An energy line is an avenue, or a current. You can ride it to any destination. A line of thought, for instance, can take you into uncharted territory. In this instance, a line of thought is one form of energy. Reality, itself, is also a line of energy. Hence, the Toltec lineage—thereby the Toltec world—is also a line. This line has been evolving for thousands of years as it has been cultivated by generation after generation of Toltecs.

From another angle, generation after generation of Toltecs have become increasingly aware of this energy line. Whether you regard evolution as something that is built from one moment to the next, or as something that is already in place and you become increasingly aware of that which already *is*, the effect is the same: riding it requires purposeful effort.

Links. Energy links are lines that connect one energy to another. If you think about someone, for example, you're establishing a link with that person. If you touch something, you've formed a physical-energy link with it.

State. An identifiable experience is a state of energy. You might be tired, hungry, sad, or angry. A state may also be considered a mood. You can be in the mood of a nincompoop, or in the state of a ranger's impeccability. You might be in a state of perennial slumber, or in a realized state of freedom.

Stage. This is a wider perspective of energy states. If you're just beginning your quest to freedom, you are in one stage of growth. If you've been traveling for a while, and have realized more complex portions of the craft, you're in a different stage. It's like a level of *being*, whereas a state helps you build a stage.

Seed. The initial impetus to something, the first recognition of something becoming actualized, is a seed. When you were young, and your teacher told you 2 + 2 = 4, a seed of arithmetic was planted within you. Seeds contain potential as they hold the blueprint for entire lines, states, and stages of energy to blossom.

Influence. Whatever affects something else holds influence. The heat from burning wood in a fireplace, for example, influences the temperature of a room. Certain kinds of mind-altering drugs influence perception. They also influence the physical body; whereas they may offer glimpses into human potentials of perception, they also take a toll.

Then, too, if you hang out with criminals, you'll be influenced by them and their energy. If you're associated with people who are impeccable, you'll be influenced as such.

Entrainment. This is a particular kind of influence. Your arithmetic teacher, relating to an earlier example, entrained your thinking along the energy line of addition. The Hemi-Sync™ technology of TMI entrains perception into new potentials of perception, thereby helping potential become realized.

Intent. The ability to produce shifts of awareness results from the application of intent (*Fire*, 218). Through intent you shift, entrain, and then restabilize your perception to a given location. You intend to walk, for example, or to *see* the Eagle's emanations. Like many features of the Toltec world, intent is beyond understanding. It's an effect, an ability. The pure understanding of intent is that you can intend, and intending produces results. No further clarification required.

Field. From a Toltec perspective, there are three fields of energy, simply labeled the first, second, and third fields. In his books, Castaneda refers to these as the first, second, and third attentions (*Fire*, 46). To help a person grasp this, initially the first field is defined as physical energy, the second as nonphysical energy, and the third as a state of energy beyond the human condition.

Later, when a person has been sufficiently influenced by various energies, and a person begins to *see* the world as energy, the definitions change. The first field then relates to what is known, what has been learned and realized; the second to potential, or that which waits to be realized; and the third to potential that cannot be realized within the normal human state.

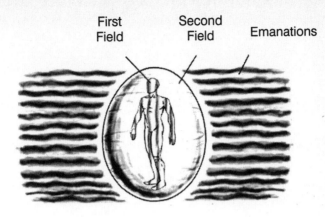

First Field   Second Field   Emanations

Energy Fields

First Field: Physical energies; Order; the Known World.
Second Field: Nonphysical energies; the Unknown World.
Third Field: Outside the human condition; the Unknowable.
Emanations: Energy lines emanating from the Eagle.

Conditional. This is the energy of form. Reality is a state of energy that we have conditioned ourselves to perceive, our *inventory* of what's out there. In fact, perception is usually restricted to what you believe you're entitled to perceive. Even *seeing* the Eagle and its emanations is based on accepting, and being influenced by, the condition that they exist in the first place. In ordinary reality, we have accepted the condition that the world is made up of material, concrete objects. From there, we build aircraft and automobiles to enable our energy fields to travel. In a nonordinary Toltec world, you learn to travel by transforming the potential of advanced dreaming into realization. Indeed, learning to transport their bodies into other dimensions was one of the ancients' great discoveries (*Fire,* 92). To do this, you have to buy into the nonordinary conditions of perception. Hence, you allow a nonordinary philosophy to entrain your energy, and thereby your perception, along a new line.

The conditions of an energy line form the boundaries of what may be realized. As don Juan says, the abstract cores—the underlying conditions of the Toltec world—form a blueprint for a complete sequence of events. One abstract is that Spirit can manifest itself to an individual; in other words, Spirit communicates with us. However, without actually participating with this condition it remains in the realm of potential. Only by behaving in accordance with it does it become realized (*Silence*, 6–7). This, in turn, influences us to realize that we are connected with Spirit. By participating with several abstracts, you grow into new stages.

Natural. This is energy that has no form and yet contains form. Your total energy field is natural to you. By realizing its potential, you keep growing beyond the conditions that you encounter at each stage. Evolving to the state of freedom means that you have grown beyond the conditional energies of ordinary and nonordinary worlds. You can *be* without the context and guidance a worldview provides. Maturation along a path of freedom is remembering, or awakening unto, your natural state. Having a natural field means you are fully connected to—and are in harmony with—Spirit.

First Second
Field Field Emanations

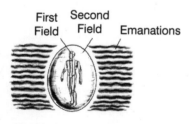 

Conditional Energy Field   Natural Energy Field

The diagram on the left symbolizes how a conditional energy field removes perception from the emanations, and, therefore, from the flow of Spirit. A natural energy field represents having harmony and balance with the world at large.

Tracking. This relates to the first energy field. Since the first field pertains to the physical world, tracking deals with handling this energy—especially your interactions with people. Tracking also relates to stability. Accordingly, using a system to evolve your awareness is a form of tracking, of taking directed and purposeful steps.

Dreaming. This is a technical term relating to behavior in the second energy field. It does not relate to normal dreaming. When you access the second energy field, you are dreaming. Toltecs use a number of meditative-like exercises to dream. Dreaming may also be produced by listening to Hemi-Sync™, as it entrains your awareness to the second field. Once in dreaming, you may intend virtually anything.

Tracking and dreaming are integral components of a Toltec path, as they are the practices that give you a crack at freedom (*Fire*, 20). Therefore, each is discussed later in this book. For now, let's make all this talk about energy a little more personal as we look at what you have in your energy body.

The Energy Body

Through *seeing*, it is obvious that there is a nonphysical energy that surrounds and permeates the physical body. When first *seeing* the energy body, people often *see* a haze, a very soft rain of light, or a band of white energy around a person's physical body. Continued practice yields the perception of an oblong ball of light. Within this ball are ropes of light that resemble a bundle of optical fibers. Don Juan says that the ancient Toltecs discovered that this glowing energy—the energy body itself—was responsible for awareness. He also says that when Toltecs *see* a human "they *see* a giant, luminous shape that floats, making as it moves, a deep furrow in the energy of the earth, just as if the luminous shape had a taproot that was dragging" (*Dreaming*, 8, 5).

The energy body belongs to a specific band of energy; naturally enough, the human emanation of the Eagle. Within this band are a number of narrower bands, just as an AM or FM radio band has numerous stations. Put another way, just as the physical body has various systems (respiratory, circulatory, skeletal, etc.) the energy body has distinct features. Here are a few:

Right side. For most people the right side of the energy body is a narrow slice of the entire body. It is handled as the tracking, or known, world. Toltecs deliberately expand their known world, and therefore their right side becomes larger than normal.

Left side. The remaining area of the energy body contains the unknown, or dreaming, energies.

Regions. Don Juan says that the energy body is a bundle of several regions. Some regions hold awareness of organic life, some inorganic life, and some containing no life, as they are solely organizations of energy. Only one of these regions is what we associate with human activity (*Fire*, 161–165). Another, known as the *inorganic world*, is touched on in the chapter "In Your Dreams."

Core. By accessing all regions, Toltecs light up their entire energy body. One tracking maneuver to do this is to remain aware of yourself without being consumed by your sense of having a self. For this, you need a reference point. If your reference is the core of your energy, which is a direct emanation of Spirit, and you start with an assumption that you are only on the surface of what's possible, you stay open. Thus, you can remain aware without being consumed.

In essence, there is no actual core. Arriving at your core is a way of saying you've awakened your entire energy body, and your deepest connection to source energy. Therefore, all of these terms are a way to give you conditions—nonordinary conditions—from which to engage advanced human potential. Realizing them catapults you into even greater capabilities. The conditions offer you a reference for the quest. They help you understand that the core is really the essence of the human emanation. Accordingly, your identity then becomes the Eagle. The more you become aware of the Eagle, the greater chance you stand of surpassing that energy. You may then "go past" the Eagle to freedom.

Uniformity. This pertains to the overall shape of the energy body. Don Juan maintains that this shape changes over time (*Dreaming*, 5). Hence, uniformity directly relates to evolution. As the human emanations becomes more realized, the energy body changes form, and thereby causes human awareness to change. From another angle, as humans stimulate their energy bodies, the body changes, more of the human emanation becomes realized, and evolution occurs.

Cohesion. The pattern of energy inside the energy body is cohesion. While the Eagle bestows awareness through its emanations, exactly what is perceived by the individual occurs through cohesion. It is an energetic signature, a pattern of energy that perceives similar patterns. So what you experience throughout the day reflects your cohesion (*Fire*, 163; *Dreaming*, 40).

Your cohesion also changes throughout the day. You might get angry, tired, pumped up, or glued to a television. Different cultures have slightly different cohesions. However, these variations are all very minor changes. They might even be thought of as fluctuations within one cohesion, and this one cohesion is known as "reality." So within a cohesion are many options.

While several regions exist within the energy body, cohesion typically brings our attention to only one: the ordinary human region. But change cohesion and you change perception. Change it enough and you enter new worlds. When don Juan turns into a crow, for instance, he reconfigures his energy. And the capacity for this marvel, he insists, rests within the personal energy body (*Dreaming*, 217). How's that for an option?

Focal point. Cohesion can be measured or identified by the location of the focal point, which Castaneda refers to as the *assemblage point*. Awareness occurs, says don Juan, through the pressure of the Eagle's emanations on the energy body. This pressure produces an alignment of energy lines inside the energy body with those outside of it. This alignment then energizes a specific spot on or within the energy body. This spot is the focal point, or where perception is focused or assembled (*Fire*, 115).

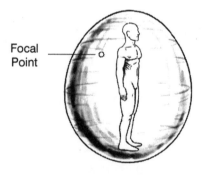

Focal Point

The Focal Point

The focal point represents an alignment of energies
inside and outside the energy body.

The focal point indicates a specific cohesion. Change cohesion and you change the location of the focal point. Sleep produces a natural shift in cohesion from the right side to accenting the left side, from the physical into the nonphysical regions. When this occurs, you *see* a corresponding shift of the focal point.

Throughout the course of a day, the focal point tends to flop around—albeit in small measure. For many, it may quiver in place. This instability results from not having a stable relationship with the world. Developing tracking is one way to counteract this, as tracking imbues cohesion with stability. Dreaming is also used to purposefully shift the focal point. Between the two, you learn to enter the unknown and remain stable while doing so, not unlike the effects of Hemi-Sync™. Just to speculate, perhaps psychological disorders result from larger-than-normal, and unstable, changes in cohesion.

A Shift in Cohesion Is a Shift in the Focal Point

As your energy pattern changes, your focal point also shifts.
Seeing focal point shifts is a way to
measure shifts in cohesion.

When the focal point shifts, you may initially feel disoriented. This is simply due to having no points of reference for your new awareness. Moving the focal point is like any skill. It requires time and effort. The more frequently you enter a new world, the more at ease you are with it. Therefore, the less disoriented you'll feel.

Don Juan places focal point changes into two categories: those occurring within the energy body, and the more dramatic shifts to outside of the energy body (*Dreaming*, 9). Entering the inorganic world or turning into a crow seem quite astounding. Yet these are mere changes of cohesion within the energy body. By introducing the notion that personal energy can extend outward and stabilize beyond the energy body, don Juan sets the stage for the quintessential marvel: freedom.

Inventory. Humans, like no other creature on Earth, says don Juan, take notice of what is inside their energy bodies (*Fire*, 83). In other words, we have a highly refined sense of self. However, we usually get lost in ourselves and forget about the rest of the world as we spend most of our energy reflecting to ourselves about our world. Lost within a mirror-bubble of our own making, we prattle on and on without ever going anywhere. We build a complex inventory without really challenging the content, value, or effects of it. We'll get back to this later when it is directly addressed as self-importance. Right now, the idea is that we isolate and build upon, specific elements of our reality. These items are the inventory. They are reference points within the infinity of awareness.

Boyfriends and girlfriends, patriotism, the pursuit of material wealth, the world as physical objects, reincarnation . . . all of these are pieces of an inventory. An inventory holds cohesion in place. They contain that much power. They also hold the power to hem you in, to restrain the recognition that other inventories, other cohesions, other worlds, exist. An inventory gives you things to look for; if something is not in your inventory you won't recognize it when you do perceive it.

Toltecs considerably add to their inventory when they introduce focal point shifts. Doing so automatically sets up the condition that awareness can move beyond the human region. By lighting up the entire energy body, you begin to access the third energy field. You may then move beyond humanness. The idea that this is even possible lets cohesion open up to it.

Watermarks. A watermark is a personal slice of cohesion. It is a state of energy. One Toltec couple I know refers to them as "lines in the sand."[1] For example, once you decide to do something, or not do something, as the case may be, you have created a watermark. Committing to a diet, for another example, is also a watermark. Your decisions have locked a piece of cohesion in place. From this stability you manifest your life and world.

Watermarks also help you break boundaries by giving you the stability to launch yourself in new directions, and into the unknown. As they define your life, make them carefully and with your overall evolution in mind. For example, pick the system you commit to with care. Systems are a bunch of watermarks acting as channel markers, and so they carry the power to shape your entire life. Each stage of your development consists of making a new set of watermarks; therefore, the ability to change watermarks is a sign of evolution. Just don't be wishy-washy about it. Create them with care, let them change with deliberation.

Bubble. The bubble is an effect of cohesion. It is the quality of *reflection,* as the pattern of energy within the energy body creates a bubble, a mirror of sorts. According to don Juan, what we perceive, then, is an echo, a reflection of our inventory off of the mirror-bubble (*Tales,* ch. 13). Thus the bubble translates energy into what we perceive physically, emotionally, and mentally. In short, how we interpret the world results from our thoughts bouncing back off the inside surface of the bubble. Thus, for the most part, reality is massive self-reflection.

In essence, there is no "external" or "internal." These are simply reference points used to describe how perception works. From a Toltec view, external means the Eagle's emanations, and internal relates to the self-contained energies inside the energy body. It is these self-contained energies that give rise to personal awareness. Yet remember that the energy body itself is part of an emanation. Therefore, it is by understanding the bubble that you begin to understand cohesion, and this helps you understand the force behind it all. Then you can begin transcending that force.

Since cohesion is influenced by emanations, the bubble is as well. And so if you're not traveling with your natural energy line—your personal emanation—you experience discordance and so you suffer. On the other hand, if you're on a natural path, you stand a better chance to evolve to further awakenings and optimally to your core.

Developing a path with heart is a way to begin working with cohesion. It balances the forces inside and out. This balance automatically produces more awareness of the Eagle. Hence a path with heart escorts you to your core. Reaching your core is equivalent to lighting up your entire personal emanation, at which time inner and outer become meaningless because you're one with the emanation; therefore, one with creation. When this happens, the notion of inner and outer goes out the window. More about the path with heart is found in the chapter "Launch Pad 101."

Form and Formlessness. The human form is a tension within cohesion that affects awareness (*Second Ring,* 153). It's also a force that pins perception to the ordinary. Typically, it means we project human traits onto the world. As a result, we make God behave as though human. Or, for another example, during a storm the ocean becomes angry. I'm not saying that the ocean does not have a spirit, energy, or consciousness. I am saying that while it may have awareness, and it may act *as though* it is angry, I'm hard-pressed to think it actually has human emotions. While God may contain human qualities, God is more than human.

Release the human form and all sorts of options prevail, including Toltec practices of tracking and dreaming. In fact, tracking and dreaming dissipate the human form and set the stage for formlessness. Formlessness results from having a very fluid energy body. You can change cohesion easily. In fact, almost any influence will alter your cohesion when you're formless; for this reason, you need to have some sense of stability. Thus, having a path with heart, knowing where you want to grow, as well as having a means to do so, help.

The roles we have in our lives are very minor changes in cohesion. Yet they produce noticeable results as you feel differently, look at the world differently, and behave differently. (Consider for a moment the changes you experience when you're at work or with loved ones.) It is by becoming proficient with a number of cohesions that you awaken the energy body and formlessness occurs. As form indicates having conditions, formlessness is necessary to evolve beyond a conditional energy field to a natural one. You're then in the world but not of it. One of don Juan's apprentices, la Gorda, says that Toltecs have two primary stages in their lives: form and formless, with formlessness being the advanced stage (*Second Ring,* 264).

Human Mold. The human mold is like a cosmic Jell-o™ mold. The Eagle stamps out different patterns of energy, some of which are trees, some of which are entities from other dimensions, and some of which are human, just to name a few. As it is the essential quality of humanness, the mold is sometimes considered the source of humans (*Second Ring,* 154). In any case, it is the energy that embraces all that is human. Since the human form has us always projecting and interpreting the world in human terms, we take "all that is human" and make it "All That Is." In short, we make the human mold, God.

When Castaneda first *saw* the mold, for instance, he interpreted it as God. His experience engulfed him in unconditional love, and he felt blissfully complete. Only after don Juan repeatedly placed him in that energy did the passion of it diminish, and only then did he perceive it as the mold . Indeed, most people who have had a near-death experience return thinking they have proof positive that there is a God.[2] Don Juan thinks that these spontaneous explorations are skewed by the prevailing social thinking; that is, the widely accepted belief of God. Since the concept of the human mold (let alone its actuality) is foreign, these near-death encounters with a higher form of energy are automatically placed in a familiar context (*Fire*, 259–265).

The human mold is within the energy body, and is represented as white light. Keep in mind that white light contains all the other colors that humans perceive, such as those in rainbows. Colors are smaller emanations within the overall human emanation. Chakras, also reminiscent of rainbows, are an example of this. To put all of this another way, the mold comprises only the first and second energy fields, and the specific energies within those fields, making them the defining element of what it means to be human. Tuning in to the energy of what it means to be completely human makes you feel, by definition, utterly complete. This may be why such an experience holds such sway over perception (*Fire*, 257). Breaking out of the mold is transcending the human condition.

Currently, many books deal with entering the white light. Most people interpret their experiences as did Castaneda; that is, having met God. This possible distortion exemplifies the need to continually challenge our assumptions, especially if they are widely accepted. Viewing the mold as God, and vice versa, may be a serious error in perception if, in fact, what has been interpreted as God is indeed the human mold. Perhaps in the same manner, what is currently regarded as Spirit will prove to be a single emanation of the Eagle. Therefore, the very grand world-views we create must give way to enhance our evolution. To hold onto them because they give us a sense of artificial peace removes us from freedom's quest.

The Evolution of the Energy Body

As the first field relates to the known world, from one perspective first-field tracking energies may be considered realized energy. In turn, second-field dreaming energies may be considered potential. As you track freedom, you learn to handle tracking energies and use them to establish a foundation to explore dreaming. In other words, you use the stability of the first field to intentionally enter, explore, and develop the second field.

You also learn to handle dreaming energies and express them in your physical world. As a result, through your intent you expand the first field. That is, you have realized more of your potential. It is by hooking the first and second fields together that you evolve beyond the normal human condition. In other words, the more you stretch the first field into the second field, which is also a way of saying you have expressed more of the second field into the first, the more these terms become meaningless as you have evolved past the conditions they represent.

For example, the Eagle was previously defined as *source energy*. Well, if you have to dart past the Eagle to be free, then the Eagle isn't the source. There must be another energy of some sort in a superior, more encompassing, or more powerful relation to it. Hence we again discover the requirements and the effects of a system. One requirement is that we use it to come to terms with our lives. Specifically, it means we have defined an energy that has significant—if not total—command of our lives. Even if we don't understand, we can achieve *relation.* One effect of having this relation is that we get out of ourselves and further into creation, not just the creation of our thoughts. Another effect is that by defining the Eagle, our perception is honed along that line. Hence we think about, and eventually perceive, the Eagle and its emanations. We have thus validated the theory, and have realized the potential of the Eagle. But if we don't understand the effects of making these conditions, we can't grow beyond them.

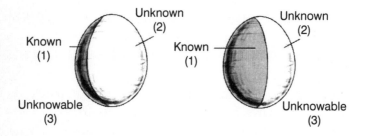

Evolving through the Energy Body

As the first energy field extends into the second field, you become more aware of the complete energy body.

To counteract the effects of their system, Toltecs incorporate within their philosophy the seed of its own destruction, or the seed of continual revelation, however you wish to view the matter. In other words, by living with the Eagle, and by fully understanding that there is no Eagle, you begin to *see* an opening for continued evolution. You use the system to generate awareness, then leave it behind when appropriate. The timing for what is appropriate is considered in the chapter "It Helps to Have a Cement Truck," which explores the stages of evolution.

By the time you have hooked the first and second fields together, you have radically transformed the way you view yourself and the world. You have grown into a unified whole where the energy body reaches out to, and connects with, the third energy field. You have then evolved beyond the normal human condition. What you find is, by definition, outside the normal human inventory. At this point, the only thing for certain is that, once there, you get to start all over again!

Conditional fields grow through the expansion of mental constructs, of enhancing a worldview. Indeed, the possibility of freedom is set up by an intellectual recognition of the potential for it. But mental energy can only take you so far. The quest becomes realized only by transforming the way you handle your complete energy. Tracking, dreaming, and intent define a way to do so. In addition, they stimulate the entire energy body. As such, they evolve the state of the energy body into new stages. Freedom, then, is entering an emanation of pure energy while maintaining your personal awareness. Hence you've retained the first-field energies of realization as well as having combined them with the more rarified energies of second-field potential. Thus you stripped away your conditional world to live constantly in the midst of potential.

To get to this point of balance requires a lifetime of concerted effort. To help you along the way, Toltecs and practitioners of other systems have isolated several distinct modes of perception. By developing these, you not only participate more completely in nonordinary worlds, but you load the dice in your favor to encounter freedom. These modes of awareness are the *cornerstones of perception* and *chakras*, and are presented in the next chapter.

3

Your
Energy
Resources

Viewing the world as energy, and studying human energy systems, lifts Toltec endeavors out of a single class of philosophy and begins to stretch that knowledge across disciplines. Working with the energy body, for example, provides a common denominator, a common reference point for the study of human energies regardless of any particular philosophy. This is because "energy" is a well-established part of the known world. Toltec practices, then, are a particular way of learning to handle energy.

Just as the physical body has different modes of perception (hearing, sight, touch, etc), so does the energy body. Eastern philosophies tend to present these as chakras, or nonphysical energy centers located in roughly a straight path along the spine. The first chakra (which relates to physical energy) is at the bottom of the spine, and the seventh (relating to spiritual awareness) is at the top of the head. These are described later in this chapter.

Another of the unique offerings of Toltec philosophy is a distinct organization of perceptual abilities. Areas of perception are scattered about the body, not in a straight line, as are the chakras. I refer to these as cornerstones, whereas don Juan refers to them as *points of our totality* (*Tales,* 99). To compare these with physical senses, for example, normal vision gives you a view of humans as having a head, two arms, two legs, and so forth. The cornerstone *seeing* gives you a view of the luminous energy body. That is, you perceive energy directly. Among the other cornerstones are reason, thinking (also known as "talking"), feeling, dreaming, and *will*.

The Cornerstones of Perception

Don Juan gives each cornerstone a specific location in the physical body. Reason and thinking, for example, are in the head. At the tip of the sternum is feeling. In the vicinity of the navel is *will*. It's an easy jump, then, to place these in the brain, the heart, and the intestines. Don Juan also says that dreaming is on the right side of the body and *seeing* is on the left, but sometimes they're both on the right side. According to la Gorda, one of don Juan's apprentices, for women dreaming is centered in the womb (*Tales,* 99; *Gift,* 140).

Eastern and western metaphysical systems often associate dreaming with the adrenal glands which are near the kidneys. Yet, sometimes dreaming is associated with the liver, which is on the right side of the body. These systems also tend to place *seeing* capabilities in the pineal area of the brain. Talking with a physician about this, I learned that the pancreas (which is on the left side of the body) and the pineal gland are both in the endocrine system. Thus they are connected. Perhaps *seeing* is activating the entire endocrine system, not just one piece of it. He also told me that sometimes the pancreas is tilted, which then places most of it on the right side of the body. Hence, there is evidence supporting don Juan's assessments.

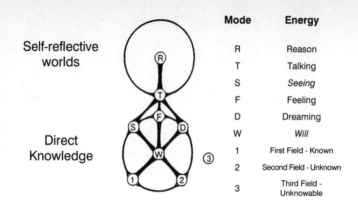

Mode	Energy
R	Reason
T	Talking
S	*Seeing*
F	Feeling
D	Dreaming
W	*Will*
1	First Field - Known
2	Second Field - Unknown
3	Third Field - Unknowable

Self-reflective worlds

Direct Knowledge

The Cornerstones of Perception

This diagram indicates the spheres of influence regarding the types of perception outlined by Toltecs.[1]

Cornerstone	Location	Perception
Reason	Brain	Organizes information from the intellect and five physical senses. Produces human-made order.
Talking	Brain	Indirect representation of the world. Translates information from the other senses.
Will	Abdomen	An integrated and focused cohesion activates this direct connection with the environment. Manages other cornerstones.
Feeling	Heart	Affective (including emotions and intuitions) sensing of self and the environment.
Dreaming	Adrenal	Nonordinary dreams, such as out-of-body states, and certain areas of the second energy field.
Seeing	Pancreas	Direct, immediate awareness of energy.
First Energy Field	Right side of the body	Realized order of the known world.
Second Energy Field	Left side of the body	Potential of the unknown.
Third Energy Field	Outside of human awareness	The unknowable. Energy that has no connection

Reason. This is a means to make order of your world. Yet this order reflects only how much energy you have learned to handle. Reason is the essence of the bubble's reflections. The tendency is to get lost in its reflection, figuring that what you look at is all there is to be seen, all there is to consider. The world then becomes very consistent as you live under the terms that you think exist. However, the world loses its mystery as you can explain darn near everything, and do so reasonably. As a result, you become very reasonable and cease becoming very mysterious. The amount of energy you have indicates how far you can stretch out your bubble. The larger the bubble, the more there is to reflect on; hence, the more order you perceive.

On the high side, when you open the door to new worlds and find yourself immersed in a sea of awareness—an ocean of infinite potential—it is reason that allows you to grasp onto something. From this raft, it also enables you to take your awareness and extend it further into the unknown. Just remember that reason, as part of the brain, is in the body. The body is not in the brain—as much as talking likes to tell you it is. Your body fully connects you with infinity, and the brain only to the portion of infinity that has been rendered reasonable.

Thinking. Thinking maintains order. You take the order generated by reason and constantly bounce that information off the inside of the bubble. Thinking, therefore, restrains awareness, keeping you in a self-reflective world. This is why don Juan considers stopping our internal dialogue an essential exercise. In fact, he considers it the key to expanding awareness (*Tales,* 233). If you don't stop your internal dialogue, you remain isolated within it. If you meet the human mold, for example, and think you've met God, then that thinking colors the entire event and your subsequent behavior. The dynamic is no different if you interpret the experience as actually having met the human mold. You have, however, given yourself an enhanced view, and room to grow beyond ordinary interpretations.

There is an order beyond thinking, and an order beyond reason. It is the order of the natural cosmos; in short, the order of pure potential. Put that in your thinking cap to help you loosen the shackles of conditional (thinking-generated) energy. Interestingly, being able to reflect on the world from a variety of angles helps you stop your internal dialogue. Perhaps this is why Castaneda had members of his team acquire a formal academic education.[2] The more you discover the relativity of worldviews, the less sway they hold. So cultivate your thinking as you learn to stop it entirely. Internal dialogue is addressed further in the chapter "Entering the Void."

Feeling. Rather than remain in the reflective world of thinking, feeling lets you tap the world directly. At the same time, it is interwoven with thinking. Your thoughts help govern how you feel, and how you feel influences your thinking. For example, if you're conditioned to think that your gender, or your ethnic race, is superior, then you'll feel and act like a bigot. But say you have a couple of experiences that get you thinking otherwise. Then perhaps you'll view males and females, or blacks and whites, as equal and thus remove superficial barriers.

In itself, educating feeling can give you widely varying experiences to expand your worldview. Through feeling, you tap the essence of a situation. You can stretch yourself beyond normal conditions, and enter new worlds. You may then feel at a loss since you've outstripped what you previously held as true. But just as you learned the ropes of your current world, you can learn the ins and outs of other worlds. It just takes time, patience, and the willingness to let go of what you think and feel is right. With sufficient experience, your feeling reorganizes itself and bestows upon you an enhanced relationship with the world. You've regained meaning.

In his best-selling book, *Emotional Intelligence*, Daniel Goleman points out the interrelationships between thinking and feeling. For example, he says that thinking plays a large role in determining our emotions and our emotions are critical for effective thinking. He also offers evidence that people often make terrible decisions because their emotional education is inadequate. Furthermore, he relates both thinking and emotions to specific areas of the brain, and says that the brain holds two intelligences: rational and emotional. It's when the two complement each other that both increase.[3]

Goleman also offers what some consider the five domains of emotional intelligence. They are recognizing your emotions, managing them, self-motivation, recognizing the emotions of others, and handling relationships. And he provides ways to educate your emotions.[4]

Toltecs also place high priority on educating emotions. Fighting fear and developing a path with heart are ways to begin handling the five domains of emotional intelligence. Other exercises include managing *projection* and developing *impeccability*. These and other exercises are presented throughout this book.

Dreaming. Dreaming enables you to directly explore your energy body. Tapping dreaming is akin to entering heightened awareness. Whereas the technology of TMI gives you a boost to do this, the goal is to enter dreaming without outside support. In turn, tracking, which emphasizes stability, allows you to integrate your dreaming travels throughout your daily life. The chapter "In Your Dreams" offers more perspectives on the dreaming cornerstone.

Seeing. To fully *see*, don Juan says you must stop the world (*Journey*, 233). And to stop the world you must stop your internal dialogue. By suspending the energy lines upheld by thinking, you allow yourself to become more aware of your complete energy body. This fullness of perception is *seeing.* As your energy body is part of an Eagle's emanation, for instance, *seeing* equates with realizing more of your nature. In this case, *seeing* is an emanation becoming aware of itself. It is the self-contained portions of the emanation (the individual energy bodies) that give rise to the Eagle's self-knowledge. The principal way to *see,* then, is to stretch yourself out and away from your thoughts about the world and into new and uncharted territory. Hence, it is by becoming nothing by becoming everything that you *see* (*Separate,* 186).

Therefore, *seeing* is highly refined projection. While it can deliver you to points inconceivable to the ordinary mind, it is an extremely enhanced form of self-reflection. This time, however, it's the Eagle reflecting instead of a dynamic occurring solely within the individual energy body. Accounting for this, don Juan says the way to avoid errors in *seeing* is to cultivate the mind. It is not that *seeing* automatically contains errors, but interpretations about *seeing* may be distorted (*Dreaming,* 8). *Seeing,* then, may paradoxically be considered an objective, unbiased, realization of the whole.

Will. Will is an energy, not a concept. It's not dedication, commitment, or persistence. It's a force. It's the binding vortex, you may say, of the cornerstones. As energy, it directly and immediately connects you with the very fluid world of energy. Indeed, managing your cohesion and your cornerstones—achieving alignments of energy—is performed with *will.*

Following a Toltec path is one way to activate *will.* The combined effect of tracking and dreaming, for instance, awakens the energy body, thereby bringing *will* to life. The procedures used to awaken *will* automatically teach you how to handle it. The stages of personal growth along a Toltec path reflect the degree to which *will* is functional. These stages are given further consideration in the chapter "It Helps to Have a Cement Truck." For now, it is important to know that activating your *will* requires extraordinary balance and concentration. The lifestyle of a ranger grooms this.

First field. As the first field is your known world, it has the energy of order. You may also think of it as that which is most familiar to you. Stepping out of reason's reflective order, you rest more easily within a natural order. The more you expand through your energy body, the more order you have at your disposal, and the more knowledge you have. One effect is that what once was unimaginable is now the order of the day. After all, your energy body is a piece of infinity, and you're realizing more of that.

Reason is the capacity for self-reflective order; thinking is the enhancement of that reflection; and the first energy field is order that has been realized out of potential energy. The more you suspend reason, therefore, the more you become adept at using the first field. Typically we behave within a very narrow margin of the energy body. Thus, we have relatively few options of behavior. It is therefore unreasonable to talk with elemental spirits, or to teleport the physical body from one place to another in the blink of an eye. Developing these capacities makes sense to a Toltec, even though they may remain flights of fancy as far as the prevailing social order goes.

Second field. Typically this is the more expansive area of the energy body. By extending the first field, you reduce the second field. That is, the unknown becomes known. A tracking perspective is that the first field is to be constantly extended into the second field. A dreaming perspective is that the second field pulls at, and thereby extends, the boundaries of the first field. In either case, you are realizing more of your innate potential.

Third field. Within ordinary and nonordinary worlds, the third field doesn't even register within awareness. In ordinary reality, perception remains isolated within the first field. The nonordinary Toltec world results from tapping the second field and balancing it with the first field. The advantage of doing this is that you have the means to deliberately exercise more of your energy body.

Then, the more your energy body comes to life, the more sensations you have of something beyond, something you just can't quite reach. The third field is this "something beyond." By firing up the entire energy body, then *willing* it into a new emanation, you perform what don Juan calls the Fire from Within. This world vanishes as your physical body disappears from this world, yet you retain individual awareness (*Fire*, 291). I think it's also possible to disappear into the second field. But if you've learned, really learned, you stand a chance of entering the third field and grasping total freedom.

The Chakras

These days, chakras have gained wide recognition, not unlike the phenomena of out-of-body experiences and reincarnation, which now appear in popular media such as in cartoons. Chakras are individual sources of energy. As such, they are forms of power. Each chakra is a vibration, an emanation. The higher along the spine a chakra is located, the higher its frequency. If you wriggle your finger quickly enough it will emit color. What color depends on the speed of the wriggle. Thus chakras extend from the base level of red through the known light spectrum to violet, the higher frequency. Their combined energy is often referred to as *kundalini*. They may also be thought of as individual dimensions, or planes of awareness. Therefore, working with these dimensions helps you achieve a more powerful relationship with your core.

Traditionally, there are seven chakras within the physical body. Combined, they produce human perception.

From a Toltec perspective, they combine to form the human region of the Eagle's emanation. To better relate these energies to the cornerstones, I use a model of ten chakras. Different systems may place different meanings on each chakra. The following model is fairly generic.

The chakras are not the cornerstones, per se, but all perceptions of the chakras may be accounted for by the cornerstones and vice versa. You may easily work with both, as each is energy based. The value of knowing both languages is that you become more flexible. Don Juan suggests cultivating your mind by expanding your options. To elaborate further:

Red. This is raw power, the baseline for physical-body and physical-world manifestations. Life as we know it is an immediate extension of this primal world. There are energy exercises where, by focusing on this root chakra, energy explodes through the entire kundalini system, pushing awareness deep into the unknown.

The first chakra is often considered the densest of energies, but I think this is projection. It may be the densest within the human region, but there are denser emanations—portions of the inorganic world, for example (*Fire,* 289).

Orange. As this chakra relates to emotions, it is somewhat associated with the feeling cornerstone. As it is the energy of emotion, it directly relates to dreaming. That is, where red is the wellspring of the physical world, orange is the wellspring of the dreaming world.

Yellow. This is the energy of discernment, of discovering and classifying. As such, this chakra compares to the reason and thinking cornerstones. With this third level of energy, you can determine how people or objects in your world relate to each other and to yourself. Not only can you perceive something external to yourself, you can compare and contrast because you can look at something from different angles.

Chakra Energies

Notice that the chakras are linear in that they
roughly follow a straight path along the spine.

Location	Color	Perception
Base of spine	Red	This energy pertains to the physical world.
Abdomen	Orange	Here we find emotional energy. Sometimes a system places sexual energy here; other systems place sexual energy in the first center.
Solar plexus	Yellow	Mental or intellectual energy. The beginning of the power of discrimination, of making refined distinctions.
Heart	Green	This energy provides for our connection with the world outside of our personal self. We begin to feel unity with the world.
Base of throat	Light blue	Communication energy. Also, this is often regarded as the entrace into more abstract regions of awareness, perhaps the intitial realization of God.
Forehead	Dark blue	Psychic energy, often referred to as the "third eye." Some systems regard this as *will*.
Crown of the head	Violet	Spiritual dimensions. The link between the personal self and more-than-human regions.
Six to eight inches above the top of the head	Enon	(The color enon is a blend of pink, violet, and metallic silver.) Perhaps we've only recently begun activating this once latent energy. It gives rise to extraterrestrials and entities existing in other dimensions.
One to two feet above the head	White	Located at the very top of the energy body, this energy contains all other emanations within the human region. It is also the human mold.
Outside of the energy body	Symbol "V"	The unknowable. Aspects of creation that do not register within normal human awareness.

Put another way, the chakras represent dimensions of awareness. The first, second, and third chakras build a three-dimensional world. When you have three points, you can play one of them off the other two. You can relate more to the world about you by comparing your experiences to two separate points of view, for instance. Thus you can obtain more information by multiplying your relationships with the world. With only two points, you can't bounce energy off of very much. The resulting information is pretty much locked in place. This is also why thinking plays such a role in emotions. Without thought, you're isolated within the wildly fluctuating energy of emotion. Thinking balances and directs that energy. This, in turn, gives you more to think about. Thus you have more control. On the other hand, by educating your emotions, you give yourself more to think about. You also begin balancing thinking and feeling.

Wanting to control your environment is the downside of the third chakra. You have such a sense of control, it's hard to let go in order to experience more . . . such as the fourth dimensional energies of the heart.

Green. This energy provides enhanced feeling. You perceive subtleties, nuances, refinements. The trick is to get out of yourself long enough to sense them. The fourth chakra opens you to worlds beyond yourself. Yet these worlds are also you.

The first three chakras represent the personal self: physical, emotional, mental aspects of separate, individual awareness. That's the sense they give. It's necessary to groom these energies to find your sense of self. From this point, you may enter worlds beyond your exclusive personal dimensions. Therefore, to get a point across, the fourth chakra takes you into, and connects you with, your environment. The more you activate the fourth chakra, the more you feel a part of the world, not separate from it.

Light blue. This is a curious energy. Located at the base of the throat, it deals with verbal communication. Charismatic people tend to have good control of this energy, and their voices are often mesmerizing. Watch yourself as you talk, and see how much balance you have expressing yourself. Are you top-heavy, speaking from your head? Is your emotional energy ruling your speech? Are you speaking from your heart? From your entire body?

Whereas the fourth chakra opened you to your environment, this energy begins to connect you with energies of a higher vibration. Feeling a strong, flexible connection with the physical world means you have balance among your first through fourth chakras. Elevating your perception of the environment, you begin to step outside the physical world and into nonphysical dimensions. For this reason, it is sometimes considered the entrance into God realization. Whereas the fourth chakra is still of this world, the fifth connects with energy out of this world.

Dark blue. Tapping this energy gives you entrance into psychic functioning. You may experience visions, telepathy, or precognition (foretelling the future). These are all aspects of *seeing*, as they indicate you're perceiving energy directly. Becoming psychic means you have greater ability to work with nonphysical energies. However, this often results in getting stuck. It's just too much fun to want to leave. You have power, and don't want to let it go. To get to freedom, you must manage the energies of the entire spectrum.

Violet. Whereas the first three chakras represent the personal self, the second set of three represents your extended environment, the world of which your self is part. The seventh energy is your entrance into worlds beyond the normal human domain. You enter heavenly dimensions of bliss, and have true mystical experiences. Since the energy is of a higher vibration, it translates to the physical body as ecstasy. It is for this reason that it is often considered the spiritual chakra.

Enon. As this energy represents extraterrestrial (ET) life, it is not of the human condition—as least as we experience it today. However, a Toltec worldview includes this chakra within the human region. Toltecs define humanness as all that is within the energy body, and this energy is within it. But it is also outside the physical body. So, for many, it is not viewed as part of the human domain.

The more we perceive ETs—be it on television shows or having a personal close encounter—the more this energy will come to life throughout all societies. The more it is energized, the more we will interact with physical ETs. That is, the more we learn to manage this energy, the more we perceive what it resonates with. So the more we resonate with ETs, the more we'll perceive them; as a result, the more we'll evolve and bring this energy into our physical selves. Then enon could very well replace the seventh chakra as the one that is at the top of our heads. At that time, *we'll* be ETs. A complete evolution of our physical bodies will have occurred.

White. This is the capstone of the energy body. It includes energies of the entire human region, including those of our evolution to a new species. This is the human mold, the composite of the entire human spectrum of energies. According to don Juan, *seeing* it time and time again is the only way to discharge its intensity, as its intensity is what distorts perception. And this distortion results in the interpretation that it is "All That Is," rather than "all that is human" (*Fire,* 260).

It is also the third energy in the third set. The seventh, eighth, and ninth chakras connect you with worlds beyond worlds. By becoming strong within yourself (the first set), developing balanced relationships with the earthly world (the second set), and gaining clarity about advanced human potential (the third set), you activate the entire energy body. As such, the first and second energy fields may also be related to the chakras. Simply, the more you activate the chakras, the more energy body you have at your disposal. Hence, the further you have stretched the first field into the second field, and the more potential you have realized.

"V." Beyond the visible light spectrum, the tenth chakra may be considered the third energy field, the unknowable. Making note of it is for the practical purpose of acknowledging that there is more to the universe than human perception.

To help you get a sense of balancing the chakras, please try the following exercise:

1. Imagine a thin plane of energy—like a flat cookie sheet—going through each chakra. You should have seven separate energies evenly stacked one on top of the next with space between them. Think about them, feel them.
2. Image each chakra moving to and fro—as though each is swinging through the plane—out the front of your physical body, then back into your body, then out your back, then back into your body, and then out the front again.
3. Stop the motion. Center yourself. Feel each chakra energy resting on the plane.
4. Now imagine each chakra moving to and fro—again as though each is swinging through the plane—but this time out the right side of your physical body, then back into your body, then out the left side, then back into your body, and then out the right side again.
5. Stop the motion. Feel your energies aligned and in harmony.

By using the cornerstones and chakras, you automatically develop more awareness. You can use your new-found abilities to develop your intellect, your emotional intelligence, and your psychic prowess. Just remember the idea is to awaken your energy body, not use your power for duplicity or greed. By managing your various energies well, you step further and further into the unknown. At the same time, you build more and more of the known.

PART II

PERSONAL
SKILLS
OF
EVOLUTION

4

ENTERING
THE
VOID

To get going along a Toltec path, you need experience. It's okay to think about it, and think about what you experience. But too much thinking locks you into a conditional field. More than anything, you need to suspend the conditions of your reality. Doing so opens you to new vistas. If you become well practiced and patient, you can break free of thought and enter a void of perception. At least it seems like a void. It is potential. And since you don't have a framework for it, it feels like a void.

Don Juan refers to this sense of voidness as *not-doing*, and I refer to it as *nonpatterning*. The void is not only a sense of things, or a lack of sense, but it also applies to sojourns into the unknown. In this light, void is pure potential. Keep in mind that in some systems *void* refers to whatever exists beyond potential. Quite an abstraction to stretch the mind, eh?

For our purposes, potential energy is nonpatterned energy. As a result, the more you exercise nonpatterning, the more you're open to potential. In contrast, the *doings* of the world are our thoughts and actions that fall into categories of what we know how to do; in short, whatever occurs as a result of having a conditional energy field. Don Juan also says that not-doing is done by the body, and that it includes stopping the world and *seeing* (*Journey*, ch. 15). Performing these skills requires suspending your conditional energy, plus tapping potential.

So that you may better learn nonpatterning, here's a chapter full of perspectives and exercises that will help you manage your energy resources. In a manner, all are meditations. They all require suspending judgment regarding the outcome. They are pauses to allow something deeper within to surface.

Accept Your Fate. Accepting your fate is a common theme throughout don Juan's teachings. You meet your life (and death) head-on, living the challenges that Spirit sets on your path. In a nutshell, what manifests in front of you is an effect of your cohesion. Therefore, accepting your fate allows you to work with and through these reflections to build a stronger energy body. This lets you connect further with Spirit.

As mentioned in the last chapter, the more you control your energy body's resources, the more control you have in a variety of ways. Don Genaro, a close friend of don Juan's, for example, could teleport his awareness over great physical distance. He had that much control. As don Juan explained to Castaneda, don Genaro was a person of knowledge and therefore had the ability to control himself without controlling anything else. He *saw* people and events, decided his course of action, and then accepted his fate (*Tales*, 63–64). In the chapter "Spellbound" we take a closer look at fate when the notion of *karma* arises.

Accessibility. The overriding consideration here is that you yield to Spirit. Ultimately, the idea is to serve only one master: Spirit, or God, whatever your terminology. In general application, it means you access energy. You form a link. What you link up with depends on a number of things. For example, if people are poking fun at you, and you let this get you down, you are accessible to their energies. You have slipped into their field and they'll run over you as though you were a lame jack rabbit. If you yell and scream at them uncontrollably, you're also accessible. You're allowing the circumstances to hold sway over you, and another energy is managing yours.

When you're accessible, you're not centered within. Your focus has gotten off track, and, as a result, you're subject to the pushes and pulls of any influence that comes along. Therefore, building a path with heart is one way to become more accessible to Spirit as it awakens your personal emanation of Spirit. You also need to set your priorities. For example, are you willing to endure the slings and arrows of your fellow humans as you withdraw your allegiance to the social order so that you may pledge allegiance to God?

In addition, don Juan says that worrying automatically makes you accessible (*Journey*, 95). You have lost immediate control of your energies as you center yourself in the thoughts and feelings about what others think about you. Constructive reflection, according to Goleman, is not worry. Indeed, it is a way to cultivate emotional intelligence.[1]

Body Knowledge. Healing my ulcer taught me that many of the ills today, be they environmental or personal, stem from not paying attention to the world and to ourselves—and paying attention by using our bodies. We have lost ourselves in a symbolic world that has no direct connection to what's really going on (whatever that is). Mental reflections cannot account for everything in the world. But since our physical bodies connect with the world, we simply need to connect with our bodies. By doing so, we tap an order that transcends the intellect.

Listen to your body. If you have an ache, for example, feel it. Let the energy from it fully enter your awareness. This allows you to discover why you ache. If you're near-sighted, ask yourself why you won't look into the distance . . . clearly. Don't get me wrong, I'm not prescribing a cure-all. However, I am very much saying that, from personal experience, listening to your body provides more knowledge than most people can imagine.

Will activates when you have sufficiently stimulated your cohesion, and have integrated that energy into your daily world. The only way I know to do this is to own up to your body knowledge. Through it, you *know* that the first and second energy fields are not separate. They are distinct categories of energy, but they are also interwoven. In the final analysis they are one and the same. Making the distinction between them, however, serves to call your attention to different worlds and ways of perceiving. Cultivating the distinctions helps you evolve. Leaving the distinctions behind helps you evolve further.

All the exercises and perspectives in this chapter facilitate learning body knowledge. In addition, exercise appropriately, eat well, and engage in positive, life-affirming activities.

Death, the Adviser. Ultimate terror, to me, would be a person on his deathbed realizing he had never lived his life. When you're in touch with your death, you're in touch with the fullness of life. Knowing that someday you'll be out of time gives you the gumption to make use of all the time you have.

You may also use death to help you create watermarks. Remember, a watermark is a stable aspect of cohesion. It's not something you want to waver to and fro about. It's your stability, and something you're placing your life on the line for. Keeping your friends, for instance, might be a watermark. You have firmly decided that they'll remain in your life, and that you are there for them regardless of the circumstances. A group of watermarks defines who you are. Again, your behavior, not your talk, is your reference. A person might talk lovingly about his friends, then behave contrary to that. Put another way, your watermarks are your life. And you can use your death to help you find them.

Fluidity. It is by matching personal energies with the Eagle's emanations, says don Juan, that we become "fluid, forever in motion, eternal" (*Fire*, 68). Thus, becoming fluid and flexible is building that type of connection with Spirit. Fluidity helps keep perception open, and lets cohesion shift. This doesn't mean to be wishy-washy. Watermarks provide you stability, balance, and strength, and in relation to flexibility, they let you shift easily while remaining steadfast.

Humans tend to have fixations, and these equate to pieces of cohesion that are locked in place. Fixations differ from watermarks in that watermarks are deliberately forged from strength and flexibility; fixations are more like barnacles. Fluidity gracefully pries away the barnacles and lets watermarks breathe life into the energy body.

Our urge to hang on to things is immense. It is a force in itself. But letting go is the only way to explore new horizons, and to tackle the unknown. Otherwise, you remain fixated by only that which you know. Or more accurately, what you think you know. By letting go, by becoming fluid, you discover your innate self—your God-created self, not the society-created self most people walk around in. To begin working with this notion, ask yourself: "When I let go, what remains?"

Compared to the quest of sparking an awareness of your core energy, it's easy to let all else go. There is no greater adventure.

Gazing. Gazing is an energy-body posture that enables you to tap the second field. A form of nonpatterning, it's a direct avenue into *seeing*. It involves letting go. It requires fluidity. In one motion, you must simultaneously relax and remain very attentive. You then gaze at, and relax into, the energy field you're studying.

Put another way, gazing lets you merge your first and second fields, thereby making a direct connection with energy. As you match (or align) your energy body with energies at large, you begin to *see*. You might say gazing helps the energy body become more supple. As such, it helps you explore and strengthen your awareness with a field of energy totally distinct from the field of physical energy you're most familiar with. For this reason, don't gaze while driving or operating machinery, because you might remove yourself too far from the ordinary. You can, however, gaze while talking with people. As you gaze at their energy bodies, for instance, let your speech arise easily and naturally.

You can gaze at darn near anything. Don Juan's apprentices, for example, gazed at trees, clouds, shadows, rain, and other forms of nature (*Second Ring*, 285–287). You can also gaze at music, traffic, art, and the air itself. Gazing at a specific thing acts as an aid to hold your attention so that you can eventually learn to gaze at anything, anywhere.

To begin:

1. Relax. Try to be nonattached to anything you perceive.
2. Establish an intent to gaze. Summon your reserves and focus on shifting your perception.
3. Don't focus on the world as you normally might. Don't, for example, pick out an object and then look at it. Let your eyes go soft, unfocused.
4. Feel your body merge with the world. Remain centered within your body.
5. If you see a haze of light, or swirling dots—energy swirls, as they're often called—let them be. Don't focus on them or you'll go back into physical-world focus. The light is the second field breaking into your awareness. Later, when you have gained more experience, you can focus on

the light and it won't disappear. But until you train your eyes, and your body, your normal habits of perception will take you back to your ordinary world.

Inaccessibility. This is one of the most difficult lessons around. It is the balance to accessibility. Accessibility to the world means you're not centered in the here and now, and you float around, subject to stray influences. Remember that your accessibility to Spirit comes when you're in some way connected with Spirit and are allowing that force to govern you, to hold sway over your decisions. Accessibility to all other energies is what requires counterbalancing. You have to learn by trial-and-error and trial-and-success when to be accessible, and when not. According to don Juan, this is a quintessential lesson for becoming a hunter, whether you're hunting food or knowledge (*Journey,* ch. 7).

Inaccessibility does not mean to exclude energies, or to block awareness. You need to be aware of what's going on all about you. But you also need to remain connected primarily to Spirit as potential, rather than to the features of Spirit, such as people, Earth, and other dimensions. When you're accessible, you lose energy. It drains right out of you. For example, if you're overly concerned about fixing your car, what your spouse wants, or how work is going, you incorrectly connect with those energies and those energies pull you off your mark and away from yourself. As a result, energy flows from you and into other energy lines.

You are inaccessible when your cohesion is stable, integrated, and energy flows to and with Spirit. You can then correctly connect with other energies as you can measure and assess them more objectively. Then you may play out the rhythm of your own life. Following your path with heart helps you avoid entanglements with the energy lines of others. Also, don't contend with the dream of daily life. Know your role in it, then let it all go.

Inaccessibility also paves the way to enter other dimensions. The fewer energy connections you have with this world, the more energy you have to head elsewhere. Dreaming, for instance, is a controlled shift into the second field. Such a shift opens the doors to other worlds, some of which are inhabited by creatures of one kind or another. Remaining inaccessible helps you explore these worlds, as well as return to this one more readily.

The combination of accessibility and inaccessibility acts like a power generator at a dam. You manage your resources to give yourself energy reserves, as you let energy flow in a controlled manner to produce even more energy. Again, the trick is knowing when to open the gates or keep them closed. Other exercises in this chapter support this dynamic duo of energy management.

Internal Dialogue. Okay, spend some extra time with this one. It's important. For our purposes here, your internal dialogue has two major components: interpretation and projection.

Interpretations result from reflections within your cohesion, or the bubble of perception. For example, if your focal point is at the position "behavioral psychology," when you see people acting like they own the world, you'll say to yourself that those people have been conditioned by their upbringing and by society to behave like that. If your focal point is at "Toltec theory," you'll say to yourself that those people have too rigid a conditional energy field. If your focal point is at "mechanistic world," then the world is composed of material objects. If your focal point is at "Toltec theory," then the world is viewed as energy.

When trying to get a handle on the quest for freedom, being in one focal point position or another is not necessarily a problem. All positions yield truth, at least truth as viewed from within the cohesion a focal point position represents. Experiencing many cohesions only adds momentum to your quest. There can be a problem of fixation, however, of having a conditional energy field dictate your options. This is why stopping the internal dialogue is so important, as doing so lets you suspend conditional fields. Energy outside the conditional fields may then enter your awareness. Indeed, the essence of nonpatterning is suspending conditional fields and tapping potential, as potential is nonpatterned energy.

Every time you label something—an event, a person's behavior, a theory—you're interpreting the world. You give energy to keeping your cohesion in exactly the same pattern that gave rise to the interpretation in the first place. The magic of maintaining a cohesion is that entire realities are built from sharing with others a similar focal point position. The dark side is that we can lose the mystery of the world.

Interpretation is a form of projection, which is "attributing one's own traits or attitudes to others."[2] As such, projection is an effect of the bubble of perception. Your ideas bounce off the inside of the bubble, reflecting your ideas right back at you. Indeed, you can tell what cohesion people have—where they're at, so to speak—by what they talk about, what they criticize or condone, and what kind of solutions to problems they offer; in short, how they think the world is, as their cohesion determines the world they inhabit.

A common measure of projection is emotional response. If a person responds heatedly, for instance, the odds of projection being in play are substantial. Say a person yells at you and says that you're trying to control other people. More than likely, you've hit a nerve and the other person has that dynamic occurring within himself or herself. The other person may not even recognize the behavior; indeed, usually not. In general, therefore, if you find someone going on and on about another person, then you can pretty much figure that the person speaking is that way. More precisely, the person's cohesion is in the same pattern.

Even more compelling than emotional flareups, is the *emotional continuity* worldviews provide. You can think you're out of the throes of projection by controlling your thoughts, but realities are also held together by emotional links, emotional commitments. How you think the world is, is often bound by how you feel the world is. This is why all heck breaks loose when you challenge the underpinnings of another's reality. People may think they're mentally agile and therefore stable, but start tapping on their emotional connections and you'll get emotion!

On top of all this consider *physical continuity*, or projection arising from the very physical world we inhabit. Our familiarity with trees, rocks, clouds, and all other physical-world elements exerts pressure to keep the focal point stable. Shifting cohesion into different worlds shatters this continuity. Tracking skills prepare you to handle such a shift; dreaming gives you the option to actually do it.

In each case, it's the internal dialogue that aims and maintains perception; that is, offers continuity. Hence, stopping the internal dialogue is the best way to handle projection. Without thoughts, cohesion slips and slides. Indeed, don Juan tells Castaneda that the first thing he taught him was that the world is just thoughts, a mere description; evolving beyond those thoughts is a matter of stopping the flow of that energy.

Relaxation, observation, nonattachment all support stopping the internal dialogue, the most important skill a Toltec has (*Tales,* 231). You may find techniques to perform this in Castaneda's, Victor Sanchez's, and my books.[3] (Research is a form of tracking. If you're serious about making the journey, you'll track down any skills you need to make it.)

Once you stop your inner dialogue, you open the door to *will,* the force that helps you stabilize your world. Therefore, as you travel Toltec corridors, practice as many skills as possible. When cohesion slips and slides as a result of stopping the dialogue, you need other skills to help you remain alert and sober.

Nonattachment. Nonattachment is most often, I think, perceived as mental agility, or perhaps emotional distance. Thus a person is viewed as adept in coming up with just the right answer for the situation, or seems aloof. But nonattachment is more than this, and has wide-ranging effects. Don Juan says he existed in quiet desperation and had only ordinary needs when he temporarily lost his nonattachment (*Silence,* 208).

Without nonattachment, it's difficult to place your life on the line. The terminal velocity of life will drain you. So let me propose that you never will really have a house, a car, a relationship of your own unless you can let it all go to see what remains. For this, you need nonattachment.

When you find yourself in turmoil, nonattachment lets you assess the situation, and take appropriate steps. If you do lose your control, it helps you reclaim your power more readily. Nonattachment, then, gives you maneuverability. You're not invested in a particular outcome, so you're freer to act as you wish.

Focusing on your death, remaining inaccessible, and fluidity all assist the development of nonattachment. But don't expand this into not caring, or not feeling your connection with the world. It is not an absence of passion. It is not severing your ties. Indeed, it is an enhanced relationship with the world. As Shunryu Suzuki writes in the classic book *Zen Mind, Beginner's Mind*, it is something that can help you find the reality in each moment.[4]

Observation. Pay attention to what happens, how you feel, what you think about when you enact these exercises, or as you go through your day. Watch your thoughts. Track your emotions. Listen to yourself, to others, to the world. Indeed, listening allows new alignments of energy to occur.

It enables you to become aware of the world in different ways. It is a principal means of observation.

Through observation—of self and world—you can become a dispassionate witness to life. Again, this doesn't mean to leave passion behind. Just be nonattached to it. By choreographing several nonpatterning skills, you may better study your energies, and what behaviors build or dissipate your personal power.

Self-observation is tracking yourself. It is not looking at yourself in the mirror and being ever so pleased, or displeased, with what you find. Rather, you must establish a point of awareness away from your physical body, then observe your behavior—all of your behavior—from that outside vantage point. This promotes objectivity so that you may change your behavior as you *see* fit. Furthermore, by stepping outside of yourself, so to speak, you reduce projection.

Through observation of self and world, you'll find your path with heart because you'll discover how your energy connects naturally with the world. This is a step toward having a natural energy field.

Personal History. Our roles that make up personal history are encumbrances. When you give yourself an identity—a salesperson, a wife, a mother, a soothsayer—you place all your energies within that structure. You limit yourself. Yes, it does offer focus and continuity. And you can tell your friends what you do. But the more you do it, the less mysterious you are—the less potential you have—not only for others, but for yourself.

Not carrying around an identity lets you be more fluid. As mentioned, fluidity helps you shift cohesion. Shifting cohesion lets you light up more of your energy body. At the same time, it is a tracking exercise to shift identities, akin to *shapeshifting,* a sophisticated tracking skill of shifting cohesion to such an extent that the physical body changes form. When you change identities purposefully, you learn to stabilize different cohesions. Stabilizing remarkably different cohesions is what enabled Castaneda to shapeshift into a crow, for instance, and don Juan shift to being a decrepit old man (*Teachings,* 188; *Silence,* 164).

One way to jettison your history is to let others do it for you. How often have you been in a conversation and another person answers questions posed to you? When this happens, let the other person answer as you sit quietly while the conversation sails away into uncharted regions. It's also helpful, and often very difficult, not to be bound by the thoughts or expectations of others. When people tell you that you're a certain way, even though you know their views don't hold much water, it's still hard to remain unfettered and go about your business. But if you can do this, you'll reap interesting dividends in terms of awareness about how people behave.

Relax. Okay, now you have to relax. So go ahead and tense up over this requirement. And if you do, remain nonattached. Doing so helps you observe yourself. By observing yourself, you'll eventually notice you're no longer relaxed. Then you can let go, use your death to remind yourself what's truly important to you, become inaccessible, and then once again relax. See how these exercises bolster each other?

If you're not relaxed, you'll expend energy wantonly. Your body will have a difficult time adjusting to new energies, new cohesions. You won't apply your efforts correctly, and it will take more time than you want to achieve something. If you remain nonattached and relaxed, though it may seem like your learning is taking longer, it really isn't. You're just more aware of yourself learning.

To relax, let any pressures you feel settle throughout your body. Allow your cohesion to gradually shift to the focal point position known as "relaxation." Pay attention to yourself; observe yourself. Let go, step by step, down and throughout your body. Counting one to ten as you let go of tension in different parts of your body is a popular meditation. In addition, accepting your fate and remaining accessible to Spirit help establish priorities. These relationships are your energetic posture. With the correct posture, you automatically relax into your life, and then live it without recrimination and with joy and abandon.

Responsibility. It's not only what you think, but how you behave, that demonstrates what you know. So learning is a change in behavior. It's up to you to decide how to express your knowledge. Don't hold others responsible for any aspect of your life. To do so gives away your power. And without personal power, you can never take charge of your life and make course corrections.

A system and a teacher can carry you only so far. Good ones help you get on your way, no doubt about that. But to account for the evolution of a system, a way, *and* yourself, you need to take full stock of your resources. Come the devil, high water, or the disparaging remarks of others, to lay your life on the line you must be responsible.

Routines. Your habits keep your cohesion stable. So in this regard, they are highly beneficial. Otherwise, your mind would be off and away all the time, which is generally the case anyway. Routines, however, also dull awareness. They keep you focused on the same things, day in and day out. This is why don Juan taught Castaneda to hunt for food by having him disarrange his habits. Castaneda had to let go, tune more into his body, and develop a new set of skills to be successful. It was this new set of skills that became a new set of habits. Don Juan then guided Castaneda into using his new skills to hunt knowledge habitually (*Journey,* ch. 6).

There are physical, emotional, and mental habits—each influencing the others. Driving the same route to work is a physical habit, consistently getting angry when someone says she disagrees with you is an emotional habit, and always thinking that the world is just physical (even if it is considered physical energy) is a mental habit. Each of these habits reflects an energy pattern within the energy body; in other words, each habit originates from cohesion. Fluidity is what you're aiming for when you begin your habit-breaking endeavors.

An ordinary conditional energy field is built through a set of habits, such as looking at the world as a set of objects, or feeling that there is nothing beyond this world. A nonordinary conditional energy field is built through another set of habits, like gazing for elemental spirits and shapeshifting. The value of building a new conditional energy field is that by doing so you learn the ins and outs of conditional energy. By applying this knowledge, you stand a chance of building a natural energy field. Only with a natural field do you stand a chance of entering the third energy field.

5

STABILITY
STABILIZES

Tracking is a relatively recent Toltec innovation. It arose out of need. It seems that the old cycle of Toltecs lost themselves in an excess of greed, manipulation of others, and accumulation of powers. Due to their extermination resulting from the Indian wars and the Inquisition, the remnant went underground and revamped their errant ways. They redirected their quest toward freedom, not enhancement of the self. Tracking, as taught by don Juan, offers the balance and the stability to pursue the greater quest for personal evolution (*Fire,* 166–173).

Like the tracking skills in the previous chapter, those in this chapter also help you manage your energy resources. Not only do they open you up, tracking skills help you find and plug energy leaks. Doing so is what brings about stability and peace of mind. The more you perform these skills, the more you develop a lifestyle that supports evolution. It's not always fun and games. In fact, it's downright hard work. So be patient. It takes time before you begin to get a handle on this lifestyle, and you'll find enough frustration without bringing it upon yourself.

You need a firm foundation to enter the unknown, whether you're exploring the outer reaches of the first field, or journeying into the second field. In short, you need stability of mind and purpose. While tracking promotes fluidity, stamina, resourcefulness, and resilience, the gist of the whole matter is obtaining sobriety. In this light, here are several aspects of tracking.

Alignment. A main tenet of the Toltec worldview is that alignments of energy produce perception. When the energies of an emanation intersect energies within the energy body, a cohesion is produced, and perception occurs. The location of the focal point is an indication of what manner of alignment has occurred (*Dreaming,* 7). In very general terms, if it's on the right side of the energy body, you're attentive to the physical world. If it's on the left side, you're dreaming. Therefore, to have stable perception, your cohesion must be stable. Otherwise, you'll experience a myriad meaningless shapes and sensations. For instance, ordinary dreams tend to come and go, and be very unmanageable. This means the dreaming cohesion is not stable, and therefore the focal point jitters about.

Gazing places cohesion in neutral. It lets you open up to new patterns of energy, new cohesions. Intent, on the other hand, is the stabilizer. It's what connects and binds the energies that are aligning themselves. Intent, therefore, produces stability.

Balance. The more your cohesion shifts, the more your world becomes very fluid. All sorts of things might happen—exactly what is up to you and your energy. To deal with this, you must continually adjust and adapt. This is where balance comes in. It's like a combination of patience, awareness, perseverance, and fluidity. Not to mention knowing where you want to go, what your priorities are, and what you aim to do along the way. Right, the balance of a juggling act.

A core ingredient of balance is being *grounded*. This doesn't mean you settle down, buy a house, raise a family, and pull in lots of money every year. While you may or may not have the American Dream as part of your path with heart, it means you can relate to it and to those who are dreaming it. In addition, being grounded doesn't mean you behave in a certain manner, like eating with the right utensils and cleaning up after yourself. It means you don't trash the world about you. It doesn't mean you are the embodiment of all that is good in the world. It means you have your own life, your own solid sense of yourself.

It also means you're experiencing a complete flow of energy. No matter whether you're focused in the first or second field, you're centered within yourself, and have a relaxed yet attentive way about you. In other words, you're solid in the moment, as well as open to what comes next.

And what comes next is moving to higher ground. Being grounded for one may not be the same for another. Plus, solid footing must be obtained at each step of the way. So you don't get to indulge in being spiritual, being a Toltec, or being a cool dude on the way to enlightenment. You do get to apply all of your knowledge toward making your own way with as much grace as you can summon at any given moment.

Controlled Folly. What you say about the world is not all that important. How you behave, and what you can actually do, is. One of the things don Juan gained from following a Toltec path was to *see*, and *see* very well. From this, he learned that nothing matters. Yet he chooses to act as though everything matters to him. In his own words, this is controlled folly. And he indicates that if another person learns to *see*, then to that person everything might matter. This is also controlled folly (*Separate*, 106).

By don Juan's reckoning, he has gone beyond all ordinary relationships with people and the world. When Castaneda challenged him to explain this lack of normal meaning in his life, don Juan said, "I go on living, though, because I have my *will*. Because I have tempered my *will* throughout my life until it's neat and wholesome and now it doesn't matter to me that nothing matters. My *will* controls the folly of my life" [italics mine] (*Separate*, 101).

This abstract relation to life is the hallmark of controlled folly. It is a blend of nonattachment, inaccessibility, accessibility to Spirit, observation, fluidity, and more. In short, it is the consolidation of all tracking skills. Controlled folly can give you your life and help you move smoothly through anything you experience.

Dissonance. Dissonance is used to shift cohesion. In other words, by placing yourself between opposing tensions, you set the stage to move the focal point. Therefore, you deliberately place yourself in the midst of turmoil. Perhaps the best example of this is having a *petty tyrant*, which is addressed later in this chapter.

Another example is the tension resulting from experiencing the Toltec world. Your thoughts may tell you that humans can't suddenly appear from another dimension. So when this occurs, thoughts, beliefs, and experience clash. This happened to me every time don Juan showed up, as he popped in clear out of the blue. He always threw me off balance, then left. Months later, just as I had regained my emotional balance, don Juan would appear out of nowhere again, say or do a few things, then leave me to regain my balance. His doing so became a significant point of reference for me. Over time, I learned not to think as much and just try to fully engage whatever experience I was having.

When people experience tension, a common response is to lash out. The tension within the energy body often produces violent behavior. This may be especially true for dreamers, as they have a hard time with physical-world stability. Dissonance becomes home territory for trackers, though, as they know it helps them better manage their energies.

Dreaming. For stable dreaming, you need a stable cohesion. For this, intent is key. If you intend to walk down a street, for instance, you'll most likely have a stable experience of "walking down a street." This is because you've learned how to handle that intent. You don't think about it, you do it. If you can handle intent a bit better, you can control your dreams. Like walking, it's a learnable skill.

In relation to tracking, dreaming is fertile ground to test and measure your steps. Dreaming is a wide-open ball game, meaning that anything can happen. Applying your controlled folly to it, however, you can use dreaming for problem solving, for learning new skills such as *seeing*, and for generally stretching the boundaries of your known world. More on dreaming is presented in later chapters.

Personal Power. This is an essential ingredient for personal evolution. It pertains to how much usable energy you have. By developing personal power, you can do all sorts of things: give psychic readings, have out-of-body experiences, manipulate others, bestow blessings on others. The idea, however, is to use your energy for your continued evolution. As such, personal power is best found by matching your energies with Spirit, not with lesser powers. Spirit opens all avenues to freedom if you simply open yourself completely to Spirit.

At the same time, personal power is there to use. You need it for intuitive guidance, which is the soft and silent voice of Spirit. You also need the energy of personal power to discover your path with heart. In all cases, whether you have just a wee bit or a huge chunk, don Juan says that a measure of impeccability is trusting it (*Journey*, 204).

Petty Tyrants. Petty tyrants plunge you into dissonance, which, again, is experienced as conflict between your thoughts about the way you think things ought to be versus the way the world really shapes up. You get to look at yourself and the world inside out. Petty tyrants help you hone your strengths and address your weaknesses. You become more secure, more stable, more in touch with what matters. For these reasons, they're great to have around.

Don Juan, for instance, had a petty tyrant who shot him and left him for dead. His teacher eventually formed a plan for him go back into the same situation to learn the ins and outs of petty tyrants. Don Juan's petty tyrant, who couldn't remember one Indian from the next, had forgotten all about the shooting incident. Fate delivered a just dessert when a horse kicked the man in the head and killed him. The great lesson here is to deal with petty tyrants without becoming one yourself. Don Juan wished the man no harm, yet Spirit supplied the justice (*Fire,* ch. 2).

Quite often, your petty tyrants are the people you work with. For instance, there is a peculiarity about some managers that causes them to inflict pain on their subordinates without ever addressing their own inadequacies. I don't know, I think this is some kind of law; it happens frequently enough to be one. Anyway, a good petty tyrant has authority over you in a situation that magnifies the energy, causing you to squirm. After all, your livelihood is probably on the line. I remember a part-time job I had where a young, inexperienced assistant manager had fun bossing me around as though giving orders were the sole reason for her existence. I called a friend of mine who is versed in Toltec literature. He had also worked in the same store and knew the person in question. I told him the story, surreptitiously looking for him to advise me to get out of the terrible situation. He replied, "You have a petty tyrant. Stay! Stay!" I did. The long and the short of it is that the situation helped me to lose just a bit more self-importance. It also helped inoculate me so that I wouldn't get as emotionally tripped up the next time I found myself trying to peacefully duel a petty tyrant.

Don Juan says that the Toltecs of the old days came up with a scheme of petty tyrants. In descending order of ability to exasperate and cause misery, they classified petty tyrants as petty tyrants, as little petty tyrants, as small-fry petty tyrants, and as teensy-weensy petty tyrants (*Fire,* 30). You can see they had loads of fun with the matter. Joining the ruckus, I developed my own scheme. I came up with headers such as *one-way artists, people of experience, rebels,* and *spiders.*

One-way artists always call attention to themselves at the expense of others. They twist words and events to suit themselves. For instance, a one-way artist quickly says "I did that" when something good unfolds, says "We did it" when someone nearby has success, and says "You did it" when there's trouble. Double standards rule the day, and you rue their company.

People of experience typically justify themselves by saying they have experience in the matter at hand, and therefore they are right. Just ask them. Naturally there are times when a person's experience shines. But as far as petty tyrants go, people of experience bend the world out of shape in order to rule.

Rebels torment others by playing a game of how wonderful they are because they think that they are bad in a good way by flying against the rules. Contrast this with heyokas, or sacred clowns. Heyokas are visionaries who work impeccably to disrupt social norms, and are a long-established part of Native American cultures. The difference between them is that rebels aim to confine others and heyokas work to liberate all.[1]

Spiders, as you might imagine, weave a delicate web to trap others. They ooze warmth and grace, and gently pull you into their domain.

In each case of petty tyrant, their guiding light is to control, to confound, to manipulate. They use all means to do so: peer pressure, anger, ridicule, paychecks, and maybe even guns.

To handle petty tyrants, enact all the tracking skills you can muster. Pay attention, let go, assess strengths and

85

weaknesses, remain inaccessible, nonattached and non-reactive, stay fluid, lose self-importance, control your folly . . . you get the picture. Rather than run screaming from the situation (which you'll want to do from time to time), use it as an obstacle course to build your personal power. Don't try to change or educate a petty tyrant. Use the occasion to deal with the world the way it is, not the way you wish it to be. Learn and adapt. There's too much waiting, too much wonderful mystery, too much power in the universe to think you can change a darn thing. If your petty tyrants want to change, let it come from their hearts, not your desire.

As you become embroiled with petty tyrants, use the external pressure on your energy body as a catalyst to shift your focal point. That is, use the situation to temper your energy body. For instance, use the pressure to create new watermarks. What do you want out of a job? Out of life? What can you live with, and what is a deal breaker? Where will you place your life on the line, and where will you gracefully exist? With whom do you want to associate, and what influences do you wish to avoid? What promotes strength and wisdom, and what entrains you to the dregs of pettiness? By encountering petty tyrants, you'll answer all of these questions, plus many more. You'll strengthen your cohesion, your *will*, your intent. So remain focused and balanced to enable a natural outcome to occur. When you learn what the petty tyrant represents within your cohesion, the situation evaporates—one way or another.

Principles. Check out the advice given to Castaneda in *The Eagle's Gift* by one of don Juan's teammates, Florinda. She outlines seven principles of tracking that consolidate various individual exercises. One principle, for example, is being willing to place your life on the line at any moment. This is another way of saying use your death as an adviser, and be responsible for your actions. Jettisoning from your life everything that is unnecessary is another principle. It equates with nonattachment and being inaccessible (*Gift*, 280–293).

Living by these principles, just like living any principled life, grooms you to behave in a certain manner; that is, it develops a certain lifestyle. Placing your life on the line to live by Toltec principles ushers you to the lifestyle of a ranger.

Recapitulation. This is a marvelous way to spiff up your energies, reclaim your power, and get yourself clear of obstructions. It discharges the energies of old habits, casts off the muck of that fight with your friend you just got into, and primes you to move deeper into the unknown. It's effective for all types of energy and works for anyone. Detailed exercises to perform it are presented in Castaneda's, Taisha Abelar's, Victor Sanchez's, and my work.[2] Here, I'd like to place it in a little more context, and answer a few questions that have been posed to me.

In most instances, this exercise uses the breath as a means to free your energy. First, inhale and bring the energy under scrutiny into full view. Then, exhale to release the binding force of it. You never lose the memory or the knowledge of the event. You just lose the fixating tension of it. One idea is that by recapitulating you discharge enough energy to be able to cruise past the tension of the Eagle as you enter the third energy field. If you don't offer up your energy, you get snared by the unrelenting force of the Eagle and your energy body is pulled apart, dissipating your awareness, squelching your perception (*Dreaming*, 149).

I have also found that the recapitulation may be used without using the breath. In dreaming, for example, you apply the intent of recapitulating and allow the energy release and rejuvenation to occur. As with most dreaming exercises, the procedure is accomplished faster than during the physical-body version. The key is intent. The best way to learn this intent is to practice the complete method, step by step. After learning the basics, experiment to find innovative ways to speed up the process.

There are also two principal schools of thought regarding how the breath is employed. You see, you inhale as you sweep your head across your chest, or, from another perspective, through your energy body. Some say sweep your head right to left. Others say it doesn't matter as, again, intent is key. In this case, it is the intent of pulling energy into your immediate awareness to process it, which is a subintent, if you will, of the overall exercise. Personally, I like to inhale starting from my right shoulder, as it has an effect of hooking me into a reference point of the first field. That is, as a tracking exercise, I ground myself in my daily world and then expand from there. I then work my way into the more subtle areas of the second field, into the unknown areas of my life. Then I exhale from left to right.

To illustrate its effects, some time ago I woke from a dream in a cold sweat. During the dream, a friend of mine was stabbing me with a knife. While I recapitulated the dream, I remembered an incident several years prior. The person in the dream had emphasized a point in our real-life conversation by shaking a knife at me. Evidently, the incident had left an indelible impression in my energy body. And I was only now discharging its energy.

Abelar indicates that you may use a formal method of making a list. This is where you list everyone you've come into contact with throughout your life. Then you recapitulate the entire list front to back, or vice versa.[3] Don Juan adds that a fluid style may be used (*Dreaming,* 150). For example, several people I know prefer a method of recapitulating whatever comes to their awareness as they enter the exercise. They also make sure to work through any of the day's turmoil to better clear their minds. Then, from time to time, they preselect an event to work with. For instance, they might chose a photograph out of an old album, then recapitulate it. Regardless of your method, I do think it's important to maintain an intent to work through each and every piece of your life. Take time to come up with your own innovations, being careful to test them thoroughly to make sure they work.

From years of practice, for example, I've come up with my own *Gunslinger* method of recapitulation. This can be done virtually anywhere, anytime. I aim my energies to peak the potential of the moment, to get the most out of the session, and then let whatever wants to surface, surface. That is, I try to plug myself fully into the moment. Then I wait for an energy that needs recapitulating to enter my awareness. It could be anything: a family dispute, a job-related problem, or even which movie I want to see. I then retrain my intent away from potential and plug fully into the energy to be recapitulated. Then, in one deft movement (which is akin to how my recapitulations occur in dreaming), I discharge that energy by letting it evaporate as though I had popped a balloon.

Whatever your method, make sure to enter, indeed fully live again, the experience you're working with. You need to discharge the fixation that that energy has on your energy body. This is what allows cohesion to shift. In fact, don Juan says that the recapitulation allows the focal point to move slowly, steadily, surely. He adds that most people can't tap dreaming because they're loaded down with heavy energy. This sludge keeps people from shifting out of their own stuff, as it were (*Dreaming*, 147–149). Indeed, it seems many people have the emotional balance of a child. We are simply never taught the ABC's of emotional intelligence. The recapitulation helps personal energy come into maturity.

Self-Importance. This is the big enchilada, the major league show, the reason a person travels a Toltec path in the first place: to get rid of self-importance.

Don Juan says that self-importance has two sides. One part consists of all that is good. It makes us stretch into the unknown and tackle challenges. The other side, and the side that we are dealing with here, consists of all that is putrid. It's what turns people into petty tyrants, and keeps perception imprisoned. Getting rid of the putrid stuff, says don Juan, is a masterful accomplishment (*Fire,* 28).

While self-importance has two sides, in essence it is a cohesion, a state of energy. Invariably, it reflects having a conditional energy field, whether it's ordinary or nonordinary.

So let's isolate two features of having a conditional field. The first is *self-enhancement.* This is where you measure yourself, reflect to yourself, about whether you're good or bad, are proficient or not, or are worthy or unworthy. The second is *self-reflection.* This is where you define and inter-pret yourself, others, and the world in general. Both self-enhancement and self-reflection must be brought under control to proceed at any stage, through any level. This is because losing self-importance opens doors of perception, frees up energy, gives you personal power, and thereby strengthens your connection with Spirit.

Self-enhancement is bolstering the ego, plain and sim-ple. People tend to invest huge amounts of energy into whatever it takes to defend themselves against the on-slaught of everything that seems to be outside of their sense of a personal self. Just let someone say you aren't the way you think you are, and then watch your reaction. One hallmark of self-enhancement, therefore, is getting irri-tated, or even angry, when someone sets forth an idea not in line with your thinking, or behaves contrary to what you feel is appropriate. One value of working with a metaphysi-cal system is that when you erupt, you have a tool to guide you through the turmoil and back to balance. For instance, you can work to regain your nonattachment, intend to remain inaccessible, and aim to lose more self-importance. In addition, Goleman points out that the ability to respond to being angry by bringing it under control is a mark of emotional intelligence.[4]

Another aspect of self-enhancement is self-righteousness, or indignation. You pump up the volume of an emotional outburst to let everyone know that you are right, no doubt about it. Indignation usually erupts when another person's cohesion doesn't match yours, as they are having different thoughts or feelings. Sometimes this mismatch of energies produces anger, which, at times, may be an effective means of communication, as it gets your point across. But to use it as such, it must be part of your tracking skills and not part of self-importance. In other words, your anger must be under control, and not occur simply from reactiveness. You want to manage your resources; you don't want to enter the kingdom of the petty tyrant.

To me, one of the most intriguing aspects of Toltec studies is the topic of self-reflection. The bottom line is that your interpretation or definition of anything, in any way, is a reflection from yourself to yourself within the bubble of perception. This has a high and a low side. By defining something, you bring it into view. By saying there is a second energy field, for instance, you may begin to perceive it, then explore it. The down side is that if you don't continually let go of your definitions, you won't remain open to the next new awareness. Shifting from an ordinary to a nonordinary conditional field, for example, takes a heap of work. The grandeur of the newfound reality can keep us interested for a lifetime. The more we become fluent with this other world, the more we stand to engage self-importance. There's great power in this. There are many prison bars as well. It is so much fun interpreting the world in grand ways, then playing with our magnificent views, that we often forget to summon the courage to go even further. To overcome these distractions, don Juan says that modern seers must create a very detailed description of their world, then laugh at it and throw it away (*Fire*, 256).

There is a special focal point position known as *no pity* that equates with having lost self-importance. Indeed, don Juan says that "self-importance is merely self-pity in disguise" (*Silence,* 171). Having no pity fosters objectivity, which you need to observe yourself and the world. As a result of shedding the world's trappings (that is, your views of the world), you can enter a state of complete wonder, complete openness, completeness.

To lose self-importance, here are a few exercises:

1. Don't judge or criticize others. You may gaze and *see* their energy bodies to assess their energy fields, but don't make yourself judge and jury. Any time your sensibilities are offended, look within yourself before you pin the tail on the other donkey. Remain vigilant for projection.
2. Don't define yourself. When you say "I am a writer," or "I am a mechanic," you structure your continuity within the margins that you've just defined. By buying into a definition of yourself, you lose yourself to that domain. Use your experiences to activate and balance your energy body, not to place yourself in a straightjacket.
3. When your self-importance surfaces, track it. Find the seeds of it. *See* what reveals itself. Then recapitulate it. Or recapitulate it to find the seeds of it.
4. Eliminating personal history helps you to not lock yourself within definitions.
5. Engage nonpatterning, often. Gaze frequently. Stop your internal (infernal) dialogue.
6. Study the effects of petty tyrants and projection. You'll soon see your own pettiness, your own sludge that keeps you from connecting with Spirit.

Strategy. In *Warfighting,* a book on applying U.S. Marine Corps strategies to the business world, General Gray, former Commandant of the Marine Corps, says, "War is an extreme trial of moral and physical strength and stamina."[5] As you may know, don Juan often relates the Toltec world to warfighting; hence, terms such as "ruthless" and "warrior." Toltec strategy, however, is not adversarial against others, as is military warfare. Modern Toltec endeavors are the struggles of finding true peace within the heart and mind. The rigors of a Toltec path, however, do echo General Gray's sentiments. You need "moral and physical strength and stamina."

To make progress, especially the progress of tracking freedom, you must align yourself strategically with your entire life; that is, you must realize you're in it for the long haul. The goal, the quest, the war, is that of freedom. Elements of the long-term strategy include tracking and dreaming, and whatever else needs to be done to zip past the Eagle to get to the third field. Employing tactics, such as erasing personal history, gazing, and losing self-importance, makes up the daily battles to claim your being. The only way to lose the war, says don Juan, is to quit. Joining the ranks of petty tyrants, for example, is a dead giveaway that you've lost. However, if you become a petty tyrant and then regain your senses, the good fight is still on. In essence, when you lose the strategy of being with Spirit, you've lost the struggle for your own heart (*Fire,* 42–43).

Don Juan also gives examples of grand maneuvers of strategy, behavior that is more far-reaching than individual exercises or tactics, called *attributes of warriorship.* Each of these maneuvers brings you closer to your core. Therefore, rather than create five-year plans (as you might normally design in a strategy), Toltecs strategize to maximize the moment at hand. These grand elements of strategy include control, discipline, patience, timing, *will,* and the petty tyrant (*Fire,* 39–42).

The gist of it is that control allows you to shift easily out of anger and regain your composure; discipline enables you to recognize the strengths and weaknesses of someone, say a petty tyrant, even when you're being pummeled by their energy; patience lets you restrain yourself, and wait for what is rightfully yours; timing reflects an exquisite intuitive sense of when to act and when not to; *will* is a defining element of your evolution to freedom, as you have earned greater control of your energy body; and the petty tyrant is the means to ensure you always have plenty of practice with strategy and tactics.

Traits, or Moods. While following a Toltec path, you'll experience many moods, or emotional energy states. Naturally you'll tap all the normal ones: love, envy, joy, sadness. . . . You'll deliberately cultivate the mood of optimism, of keeping your chin up regardless of the circumstances. Indeed, as Goleman points out, as we become more emotionally intelligent we find that hope sets achievers apart and that optimism is a good predictor for success.[6] This doesn't mean to be overly optimistic. To give a rather harsh example, optimism doesn't mean you head into battle thinking everything is peachy-keen, you're razor sharp, and there won't be any casualties. This type of thinking gets people killed. You must remain sober.

Going beyond the normal range of emotional experiences, there are moods that rangers cultivate in such a manner that they become traits, or recognizable characteristics. Get ready to throw sentimentality out the window, as the first and foremost is *ruthlessness*. I say it is foremost because this amazing single-mindedness is required to shift cohesion, and shifting cohesion is the defining behavior of Toltecs. I suppose the term does carry a ruthless flavor in itself. It's probably a carry-over from the old days when Toltecs had a free-for-all going. But if you play with it for a while, I think you'll find that it is a most appropriate term.

Viewed from another angle, ruthlessness is "a total lack of pity" (*Silence*, 153). Sobriety at its finest, ruthlessness does not cut off feeling; it enhances it. It provides energetic clarity to avoid feeling sorry for yourself. As it provides the objectivity to educate your heart, you feel optimistic that you can evolve, that you can study the world and yourself to such a keen level that the changes you make in your behavior produce successful results. Doing so is also the responsibility of the matter.

One way to cultivate ruthlessness is to use your death as your adviser. This is something that can break you out of a bad mood, such as when don Juan chastised Castaneda for acting like an idiot and wasting his life "in some stupid mood" of timidity. Being timid, says don Juan, prevents us from fully examining our lives, as it keeps us in a world of our thoughts only (*Journey,* 109–112). Using your death as an adviser can catapult you into the mood of a ranger.

The balance to ruthlessness is *kindness* (*Fire,* 12). Without kindness, having no pity will have you rolling over people as if they didn't have a right to exist. You'll get so wrapped up in your goals, your wishes, your doings that others will no longer be a consideration. This also comes under the heading of being inaccessible. As don Juan says, it is inappropriate to bend your world out of shape (*Journey,* 95). Therefore, balance is required to remain ruthless yet kind. When you start orchestrating it with other moods, the balancing act becomes even more challenging.

Therefore, you need *patience*. You need to find the balance of waiting and acting, a dance that is covered in later chapters.

The last of don Juan's four principal traits is *cunning*. If Florinda's seven principles of tracking are brought to bear, we find that a ranger is always figuring things out for himself or herself. Assessing the environment, choosing a course of action, and removing all encumbrances brings about cunning. In turn, this leads to creating strategies, which leads to innovation. As a result, you become nimble, which allows you to track the ebb and flow of Spirit.

Indulging in a mood is when you remain in a mood beyond the moment when it has left of its own accord, naturally, and your cohesion then reflects another mood.

But you cling to something else. This doesn't mean to flop around from one mood to another. That is also indulgence. It means you must pay attention to natural, deep-seated rhythms within you, the ones that move in alignment with the Eagle's emanation of evolution.

To recap, the energy of ruthlessness can be harsh, which is why it needs to be tempered with kindness. Kindness can have you all mushy inside, so it needs to be balanced with ruthlessness. Cunning can have you assessing the world and bending your findings to suit yourself, so it needs to have patience and kindness as ballast. Patience can have you waiting too long and you become lethargic. This is why the recipe needs ruthlessness and cunning. Now, all of these can be knotted together in other ways. Try to contrast and balance them to your own taste.

$$\mathscr{D} \; \mathscr{D} \; \mathscr{D}$$

When your cohesion is in a certain state of balance, your behavior automatically reflects the skills offered in the last two chapters. That is, you'll naturally lose self-importance, alter your routines, and remain fluid. In addition, your sense of these skills continually evolves. You always get better using them, and realize new ways to use them.

The effect of these skills is that when tracking and dreaming energies are in balance, cohesion is in that "certain state." From another angle, when the electrical activity of the right and left hemispheres of the brain are in harmony, cohesion is in that "certain state." From one perspective, stimulating and balancing cohesion balances hemispheric activity. The exercises of metaphysical philosophies help generate this type of cohesion. From another perspective, balancing the hemispheric activity generates a balanced cohesion. The technology of TMI, for example, delivers these results. Each approach works. You just need to apply yourself to the goal. Otherwise, your trip goes only so far.

PART III

MANIFESTING EVOLUTION

6

SPELLBOUND

This chapter presents some of the dynamics of how the energy body works, and how your perception is shaped by these influences. This section offers practical perspectives and exercises so that you may apply these mechanics toward building your life. Accordingly, let's look at three aspects of cohesion that are in play all the time: *karma*, *spells*, and *intent*.

Karma

For our purposes, karma means the energy at work in your energy body. This pertains to the behavior of energy inside the energy body, which includes the effects of energies interacting from inside and outside the energy body. In some systems, especially eastern philosophies, karma has many meanings; some of the meanings presented here may have different terms in those systems.

Karma is often considered cause and effect, "for whatsoever a man soweth, that shall he also reap."[1] In Toltec terms, how and what you sow reflects your cohesion. For example, when don Juan's petty tyrant was kicked to death by the horse, it's easy to say that that was the man's karma. He lived a violent life, and died a violent death. And he lived a violent life because of the pattern of his energy. If he had learned how to change his cohesion, he could have changed his behavior. He could have then manifested a different life.

Ordinary and nonordinary conditional energy fields are huge amounts of karma in action. The content of these energy fields—your cohesion—dictates what you perceive, how you interpret your experiences, and how you behave mentally, emotionally, and physically. Working out your karma, then, is discharging the energy patterns that lock you into any conditional field. As very intense projection, your current cohesion—your karma—calls experiences to you. The sum of everything that you experience, everything you believe, all that you curse, and all that you hold dear stems from karmic reflections of your cohesion. As you change your cohesion, you change the mirrors in your bubble of perception. As you change the mirrors, you change your karma. This changes the world you experience.

The popular metaphysical notion of "burning off karma" is simply applying yourself to the force of evolution. I think there is a natural force guiding our evolution. To use it for a boost, just tap into this energy line, and flow with it. As you do, you naturally awaken more and more of your energy body. With time, you arrive at your core.

Your core is energy that is most connected with the evolutionary force. Hence, by being a living part of that force you can perform marvels such as those of don Juan when he steps in and out of other energy fields. To get to your core, however, is no small feat. By meeting your fate head-on, by enduring the trials of petty tyrants, and by keeping yourself highly tuned to your quest, life gives you everything you need to burn away conditional energy. It seems apparent that we need to burn away quite a bit of this energy to burn with the Fire from Within. In short, burning off your karma is re-entering into the domain of Spirit. This is the work of it; this is the karma of it.

A system provides a means to hurl yourself into this quest. Losing self-importance, for example, gives you a chance to recognize the dynamics of karma; the recapitulation discharges energy blocks and rejuvenates your energy; having a petty tyrant brings your karma to a conscious level; establishing new watermarks and a path with heart ushers you into new relationships with the world; and your *unbending intent* to reach freedom guides your every step. A system provides the advantage of channel markers to help you orchestrate all these behaviors, without thinking you've made great gains when you've only given yourself more to think about.

Speaking of more to think about, beliefs and composite systems of beliefs are intriguing aspects of karma. Reality forms from a multitude of beliefs, all of which connect with and support other beliefs. When you combine individual beliefs (such as Earth is a flat world) with other beliefs (such as there are monsters waiting at the edge of the flat world) you form composites. These composites are the reality of the day.

Scientific theories, for instance, evolve by incorporating new information about the world into that which is already known and then going beyond those boundaries—and doing so while making sense of these travels into the unknown. Yet whether you're dealing with classical or contemporary theories, each view of the world is a constellation of karma, a composite of beliefs about reality. The karma of it is that we travel along the corridors of these beliefs, verify them at each and every step of the way, and then get lost in the amazing world we've built.

For example, our current beliefs that we cannot travel faster than the speed of light, and that we cannot survive death, are pieces of our contemporary, ordinary world. A Toltec nonordinary world, in contrast, holds that people are made up of energy, and that they can learn to teleport their physical bodies, to actually move them through time and space without using physical movement. In each case, ordinary and nonordinary worlds are a set of interlocking structures based on beliefs, and from which other like-minded beliefs emerge.

Any conditional field is built solely upon specific conditions, conditions that generate realities. In other words, each condition is a belief, and when you get enough of them acting together, you get an energy field. From this field, you get a reality. In a self-fulfilling prophecy, the reality is projected onto the world, then as it echoes back to you, it sustains itself and the conditional field. Put another way, reality is projected onto the mirrors of your perception. This reflection is then mistaken as truth.

Thus you can see that the process is the same whether you're in an ordinary or nonordinary conditional field. The difficulties may actually increase the more you work with a metaphysical system. You have a larger playground to roam, and it's easier to become captivated by all your new options. At the same time, a system can speed up your evolution considerably. Take the gait of power, for example. This is a technique of running at night, even over rough terrain. During my early years of studying Toltec ways, I practiced the gait in a variety of conditions: suburban yards, rocky coastlines, wooded areas, and deserts. By adopting a specific physical posture, then merging my energy body with the environment, I found it possible—indeed, exhilarating—to run at speeds contrary to ordinary reason.

The raw karma of it is that the gait offers proof positive that the physical body can be handled in a radically different way. The interpretation of the experience hinges on beliefs; again, an aspect of karma. For instance, one interpretation is that the physical body moves through time and space, albeit from an altered reference. From another angle, this altered state of consciousness stimulates the energy body and, in doing so, provides yet another perspective; that is, rather than the body moving through the world, the world moves through the body. In fact, if you continue to work with it, the gait of power escorts you to an awareness where time and space do not exist from a three-dimensional perspective. Any movement of your physical body results solely from shifts of your cohesion. As the focal point moves, you perceive an illusion of 3-D movement. That's the karma of it. And it's by participating with a metaphysical system that you generate revolutionary, evolutionary experiences to jolt your awareness out of the doldrums of any conditional field.

Considerations such as these help us understand that combining tracking skills offers a means to regulate cohesion and karma. To illustrate: If you stop your internal dialogue, you open the door to energy and awareness outside of your current beliefs and cohesion. If you remain nonattached, you can observe the interactions among beliefs, reality, and behavior. By using your death as your adviser, you summon the courage to step beyond your beliefs. Performing the gait of power offers proof that unknown energy dynamics exist. Performing all of these skills sets energy in motion to form new cohesions. Then, by steadfastly remaining accessible to Spirit, you travel an avenue toward your complete unfolding. As a result, you become complete.

Spells

Spells are the active side of karma. As such, reality is a huge spell. A form of spells, beliefs act as incantations that guide perception along specific routes. When you have enough of them, you have a reality. You're then so overwhelmed that you succumb to that energy, losing sight of a much grander world. You perpetuate the spell as you teach others the ins and outs of what you hold to be true.

When people say don Juan didn't—indeed, can't—return to this world from the third field, a spell is cast. I think that most spells are formed from good intentions, in efforts to understand the world. Yet spells also weave an energy that diabolically imprisons perception. So you might say that spells are petty tyrants. They keep perception locked up.

It was by studying Castaneda's books that I learned enough to meet a teacher. As don Juan says, by seriously practicing the tracking techniques of losing self-importance, erasing personal history, assuming responsibility, and using death as an adviser, a person generates sufficient personal power to find a teacher (*Tales,* 236–238). On the edge of death, that's what I did. I used all the techniques I could dig out of Castaneda's books to heal myself. I later moved to Tucson, where I met my teacher. These are facts. It's also a form of karma, as the entire situation resulted from trying to balance my cohesion. The way I tackled the situation, and the subsequent events, are also karmic.

To the very best of my accounting, my teacher is the same man who taught Castaneda. However, this is an interpretation. Before I hung my hat on this belief, I carefully measured the behavior of my teacher. I found his authoritative manner consistent with Castaneda's reporting of don Juan. I found that he used similar ploys of teaching, such as having me think and feel a wicked old witch was out to do me in. I also witnessed his amazing ability to step physically in and out of dimensions, a feat consistent with the abilities of Castaneda's don Juan. Then, to verify for myself that this man was or was not don Juan, I used my intuition and set up several omens, with both forms of guidance indicating he was. I even asked him if he had taught Castaneda, and he acknowledged that he did. These are facts. But because I can offer no evidence beyond this, interpretation is called into play. This is the karma of it. The continuing doubts I had about the matter are also karmic, as it was well beyond my imagination that the possibility of meeting don Juan existed.

As part of my daily discipline, however, I used my doubt to examine the situation. Doing so re-opened a doorway to don Juan's energy, once again connecting me with him, and from this I found emotional ballast. I also felt the strength of his entire lineage. I *saw* and felt its evolution. I experienced its darkness, its light, its flow of energy. As I regained a sense of my quest, I felt renewed. And, frankly, I felt as though I had broken a spell that was limiting the possibilities of don Juan's—indeed, any person's—abilities. A ranger focuses on wonder and beauty, not on limitation. Dealing with the petty tyrantness of the situation delivered positive results.

Anyway, let's get on with spells. Whether something is fact or belief is often a tenuous distinction. By studying the formation of reality, for instance, we find that our sense of history plays a vital role in spellbinding. On the twentieth anniversary of the moon landing, I remember a newscaster saying that twelve people in all of history had visited the moon. This version of history, this spell, does not account for nonordinary realities. Perhaps thousands of Toltecs, Hindus, and Taoists have visited the moon while dreaming. Maybe some of them even teleported to the moon with their physical bodies. From the perspective of metaphysics, this is equally valid history. Keep in mind that any moon landing is only one of a very small series of events. The sum of all historical perspectives carries immense energy and actively holds our cohesion in place. Accordingly, we find that history is part of the social base, and the social base is spell-casting on a mass scale. Adding to this mix is don Juan's advice for us to evolve beyond the current social base so that we, as a species, may survive (*Dreaming,* 3). Right, this is the grand karma of it.

Intent

Intent is one of those things that you can't talk about. So let's talk about it.

Odorless, colorless, and tasteless, it rules our lives. There are extremely powerful forms of intent, such as the Eagle's emanations, and there are intents of lesser intensity, such as wishing your dog wouldn't shed so much. But make no mistake, each and every form of intent is focused energy, and therefore a form of power. So even your idle remarks can produce unintended events. The popular metaphysical saying "Be careful what you say, it might come true" carries weight.

When you apply your intent, you place energy into motion. Accepting the premise that the world is made of energy, the energy of your intent forms the events of your life. As though you were Merlin, the master wizard of King Arthur's court, your intent summons the circumstances that will be realized out of potential. "You create your own reality" is another popular maxim reflecting this. You can cast your spells in or out of consciousness. You can meekly abide by the thoughts of others, or you can call forth the courage to be completely responsible for your life.

Beliefs can help you place considerable energy behind your intent. If you feel wronged, for example, your emotional energy augments your focus. You become more determined than ever to produce a desired outcome. On the other hand, beliefs may act as incantations that bind you. Regarding Earth as a material object for exploitation is a belief. Hear it enough and the spell begins to weave its magic. Repeated by your teachers, parents, bosses, and friends (who have also heard the incantation), the spell is brought to a bubble in the cauldron of perception, the chant is then accepted as something beyond belief. It has become fact. Or so it seems.

Remember that conditions form conditional energy fields; hence, conditions are the substance of spells. The karma of it is that either you remain isolated within the spell, or you use the spell to break out of all conditions. In short, you step from an ordinary reality, to a nonordinary reality, to freedom.

Intentionality is a term that is catching on these days. It means all processes surrounding and intertwined with intent. For instance, the combination of head and heart energies establishes a cohesion. Figuring out the mental ins and outs of something is the head stuff of intentionality. Feeling the ins and outs of something is the heart stuff. When they work together toward a common goal, you are focusing a double whammy of energy, and it's hard to miss the mark. You know, we're not helpless creatures. We have the power to do, to act, and to act intentionally. This is intentionality. Just be responsible, levelheaded, sober.

When you have different energies focused, and there is nothing dampening this energy (like worry, doubt, or fear), you have unbending intent. Unbending intent shifts cohesion, and then stabilizes it, thereby manifesting whatever it is you're hellbent on. For anyone, unbending intent works. To act as a ranger, it is crucial. Without it, you can never muster the energy to plow through conditional energy fields. They have too much power, and we're too spellbound by them. This is where all the tracking and dreaming skills come into play. You need to work with energy to handle energy. For, as don Juan says, only Toltecs (in this context, only those who have successfully explored intent) are able to turn feelings into intent (*Silence*, 244). The shift from being in a materialistic world to participating in a world of energy is where the work is at. It is metaphysical systems that provide the exercises, perspectives, and skills to make such a transformative shift.

The practicality of all this is that you have a way to build each and every part of your life and make it consistent with each and every other part. Layer your goals onto one another, for instance. Say your priority is to obtain freedom. A secondary goal might be to study Toltec ways. Another goal might be to commit yourself to a learning task. Then you might refine all your relationships to bolster your quest; that is, you deliberately cultivate friendships with those who share your goals and who contribute to your life. Of course, in this light, one of your relationships must be a petty tyrant! I think you get the picture. Make your entire life an expression of unbending intent.

The transformation we're addressing is dramatic, makes loads of sense when you understand it, but is something that can't be truly understood. Indeed, don Juan equates intent with silent knowledge, and says the more you cling to reason, the more elusive intent becomes. Castaneda realized that intent was beyond words, yet was available for everyone. The key ingredient to using it "belonged to those who probed it" (*Silence*, 167, 105). Getting to the point of understanding that you'll never understand is transformative. All sorts of doors then open, one of which is learning to explore intent.

Exploring intent hinges on educating yourself about the mechanics of your energy body, and the types of energy in the world about you and in your energy body. You need to learn how to recognize different energies, how to awaken them, and how to manage them skillfully. You also need to learn the effects of placing them into motion. Then, aided by a guidance system that intends for you to be free, you build a life consistent with the framework of the system. You then have a marvelous vehicle for navigating the universe. All of this takes you into the wizardly world of conscious manifesting.

7

MANIFESTLY
YOURS

It's time to put theory and discipline into motion for something practical. Let's look at a few perspectives and skills that can help you build your life; that is, manifest your goals.

Manifesting relates to your skill of managing your energy body, of consciously changing the mirrors within your bubble of perception. Nonpatterning techniques are the preliminaries to help you get a handle on this. Managing your energy body is the equivalent of managing awareness, meaning that you can manage what you're aware of, whether it is diet or entrance into other dimensions. Like any skill, there are levels of proficiency, of ability. In this light, here are a few dynamics at work and play within your energy body.

Chakras. Chakras form a network of energies within the energy body. Each is independent, each influences all others, and each influences the whole. What the heck does this mean?

As presented in chapter three, chakra energies correspond to specific perceptions. For instance, the first, or red vibrational energy, is of coarse physical matter. The second, or orange energy, is of the emotions. Since each relates to a specific function, each is independent. Hence, each is its own domain. As such, each is a bubble of perception pertaining to a specific territory of awareness. At the same time, since all chakra energies swirl within the energy body all the time, each influences the others as well as the whole of the network. So if you're always on the lookout for sex, your first and second chakras control your behavior. If you're studying at a university, your third chakra receives lots of attention. In other words, the energy given the most play entrains the others toward it, thereby influencing your overall behavior. Therefore, while the chakras may be in a straight line up the spine, they don't necessary play themselves out in a linear manner.

I came across an interesting example of this during the time I was channeling extraterrestrial intelligence in TMI's laboratory. During a series of sessions while using Hemi-Sync™, I contacted an energy that identified itself as extraterrestrial, from the Pleiades star system. Now, whether or not I actually talked with ETs might be a book in itself. But if you nonpattern the event, take it at face value without interpretation, the experience offers some valuable possibilities.

One of these is the *biocognitive interface* model of manifesting, a concept given to me by the ETs I channeled. It means the more you think about something, the more emotionally comfortable you'll become with the idea (such as with the existence of ETs). Then, the more emotionally comfortable you become, the greater likelihood that the idea will manifest in your physical world. In other words, by thinking about ETs, you become more emotionally comfortable with the notion of their existence. The more emotionally stable you become, the greater the likelihood of having contact with them. As a result, the energy works from mental to emotional to physical, the third chakra to the first.

Of course, your thinking is influenced by how your heart connects with the world, or how much psychic activity you have, or what your primary spiritual discipline is. In other words, the way you feel about something determines how or what you think about. This is especially true if you are emotionally charged about a topic, as your strong biases influence your thinking as well as your physical behavior. Plus, if you're naturally psychic, you have even more to think and feel about. So, again, all these energies play off all the others, each taking a lead role at some time or other.

As you gather experiences and integrate them, you form a base for further experience. From one cohesion, you build another, then another. From this process, you evolve. This is the biocognitive interface at work. To make it work efficiently, be careful to gather a wide range of experiences, and integrate them carefully. Using the chakra model is quite helpful because you have several energies to relate to any given experience. Simultaneously managing several facets of the energy body serves to make what you've integrated solid and lasting.

Your behavior reflects the energies you have learned to align with, and it manifests your experiences. This means you can make your behavior on each and every level (mental, emotional, physical, and spiritual) combine to better determine your overall behavior. Therefore, cultivate each chakra, then balance one with another to discover your relationships to each energy. This leads to unbending intent.

Let's look at the biocognitive interface from a different angle. As all of this talk about chakra energies plays itself out in mainstream society, more will be said and written about them. As a result, more people will recognize experiences associated with chakras. The more people acquaint themselves with chakras, the more they will be studied, leading to a greater understanding and a more detailed logic. Then, just as any subject grows in depth and breadth, this knowledge will become part and parcel of society's daily world—manifesting at work.

The essence of the biocognitive interface is that it helps you connect with your body, and therefore with the energy line of what you're manifesting. Following, or tracking, this energy delivers you to your goal.

Cohesion. Your cohesion is the pattern of energy within your energy body. This pattern reflects how your personal energy is aligned with emanations outside your energy body. This alignment translates into perception. Therefore, if you change your pattern of energy, you change what you perceive. A very minor change is walking down the street. A greater change is having an out-of-body experience. A huge change is the Fire from Within.

By deciding what you want, then applying yourself to that goal in a variety of ways, or even simply setting your mind to the task, you shift cohesion. If you lack raw determination, the biocognitive interface offers a structured approach (which is what systems are for). For example, say your goal is to become better at business. Highlighting the mental chakra, read more about it. Pick up several business magazines and check them out. Talk with businesspeople, exploring their faults, failures, and successes. The more you learn, the more your mind will relax, and the more capable you'll feel.

Then engage your business. Don't flail away at it. Approach it with a determined sense, apply what you've learned, abide by ethics you consider worthwhile, remain attentive to your intuition, and place your work in the context of your spiritual growth. Everything considered, you're working with a variety of energies toward a common goal. You then align with the energies that reflect what you've set in motion. You then begin to realize that experience. If all channels are tuned, you should realize success. If something is out of whack, you'll discover that instead. If so, retune that energy and proceed again. There are no guarantees. There are, however, potentials waiting to be realized.

Remember that your cohesion is built by, and simultaneously reflects, your worldview. From this energy pattern come your options. From your options comes your behavior. By changing your options, you change your worldview, your cohesion, your behavior, and the world you realize.

Decisions. For reasons just given, your decisions are governed by your cohesion. Plus, referring back to body knowledge, we find that a recurrent lesson from don Juan is that the body knows what is what, that it decides how, when, and where to act. Therefore, grooming body knowledge is equivalent to becoming aware of your cohesion (*Journey,* 292; *Tales,* 158).

At the same time, your decisions create cohesion. For example, watermarks form from a deliberate, line-in-the-sand decision about something that you're willing to place your life on the line for. For instance, an unwavering decision that you will, or will not, use drugs establishes a watermark that becomes a firm part of your cohesion. In this light, it is equivalent to intent. Establish enough watermarks and you have a fairly strong cohesion, especially if the watermarks all support each other; that is, if they are all aimed in the same direction of realizing a greater goal. In so doing, watermarks create a cohesion of integrity, a strong and flexible energy field of unbending intent.

To say this another way, watermarks are consciously created subcohesions. They are also parts of the whole. A watermark is one mirror among the many mirrors in the bubble of your perception, of your cohesion. Subcohesions, even if they are not watermarks, influence decisions. If you make up your mind to not smoke marijuana anymore, for instance, but find that when you're in the influence of those who do smoke you change your mind, a contrary subcohesion has determined your behavior. It made up your mind for you. To act consistently after having established a watermark is acting from knowledge. Your behavior has power since as you stabilize your watermarks, you deliberately stabilize an entire cohesion. This is what produces the changes in your outer world.

When you fall off the tuna boat—when you behave contrary to a watermark—climb back on board. It's only when you give up that you fail. Quite often you'll have a large amount of energy invested in your behaviors, even those you wish to change. When you create a watermark, you've experienced enough to know you don't want your old behavior to rule. But when you begin to act, all sorts of memories, influences, and longings rear up as the old cohesion begins to snap back in place. You'll find that bursts of energy from old cohesions, reflecting old habits that you wish to leave behind, surface and throw you off the tuna boat. Sticking with your decisions saves the day, and sometimes it may take years to fully form and use a watermark. But, the constant focus of energy that comes from holding fast to a decision supplies enough energy to offset old patterns. An unchangeable decision, says don Juan, generates unbending intent (*Silence*, 241). Unbending intent is a point of personal power. So make your decisions carefully, then don't turn back. As General Gray says, make decisions from awareness, not from habit. Keep in mind that the only thing that can change a ranger's decision is a new decision.

Once you make a decision, act. If you don't, the energy hovers in potential. As a result, it's not set fully into motion, and your decision is more difficult to realize.

In addition, consistency is the hallmark of decisive behavior. A cohesion forms bit by bit by sticking with your decisions. Each of your actions adds to, or subtracts from, the amount of energy you place into a cohesion. When you have a sufficient amount of energy you automatically create a new cohesion, often the result of having a new set of watermarks, a new set of commitments. As a result, your life is refreshed and you continue to evolve.

Expectation. Your expectations aim energy. As you think and feel in certain ways, your cohesion shifts to follow along those lines of energy. Like almost anything else, there's a high and a low side.

The high side is that your expectations help you manifest your goals. If you expect to have a positive experience, you increase the odds that something favorable will occur. If nothing happens, just remain nonattached to the outcome. Live and learn. The low side of expectations is that you might get in the way of greater manifestations. For instance, if your goal is to teleport your physical body, but you expect it to happen in a certain manner, then that expectation might prevent anything from happening at all.

Of course, sensing the potential of something, or being clear in your thoughts about it, may not be sufficient to realize it. You may need to take a few steps first. You may need to grow into it. Handled properly (and only you can determine what's proper), your expectations can assist your growth.

Intent. Intent is a mysterious force, silently weaving its way throughout your life, placing all your intentions into motion. It's a neutral force that moves to your beckoning. So it's a good thing to have your priorities in order. Otherwise, you intend the least little thing. Or perhaps you'll have a multitude of conflicting intentions which then produce a life of conflict.

Don Juan once related intent to manipulating your feelings in order to change your relationship with something. It is feelings handled with deliberation, with conviction, and with focus that produces intent (*Silence*, 230). Therefore, you can use feelings to gather sensations and use them as channel markers. From this you can determine your cohesion and alignments of energy, which are the substance of manifestation.

The result is that intent is focused, directed energy. As you create watermarks, for example, you refine your focus.

As a watermark is an alignment of energy, it automatically directs energy along the avenues it created. Several like-minded watermarks build a complete cohesion. A stable cohesion further increases focus.

There is an interesting balance with intent. If you focus too much, you squish energy away from you. If you focus too little, you lose your connection with it. In either case, you diminish the power of intent. Naturally, this reduces your ability to manifest. Moreover, when you establish an intent, get out of the way of your thoughts. Nurture intent by balancing the focus of it with body knowledge, then let the results come of their own accord.

Herein lies another value of working with a system. It helps you reduce haphazardness. It gives you interlocking tips on how to behave. This structure, combined with definite goals to measure your growth, provides support to better learn intent. You need to understand how projection works, how conditional fields affect perception, and how to manage these influences. A good system provides all this and more.

Karma. Unless you completely work through a cohesion, and discharge the energies of it, you'll keep bringing similar experiences to you. Say, for instance, you keep getting in relationships where your partner demeans you. This demeaning relationship reflects a cohesion known as "demeaning relationship." By using the recapitulation exercise, you can discharge the energy that holds this cohesion in place. You then make new watermarks that reflect your decisions not to take guff anymore, or to allow yourself not to be in that type of environment. As dysfunctional cohesions dissipate and you build new ones, you'll leave negative relationships behind, and find relationships that reflect your new set of watermarks.

Programming. All these techniques are aspects of programming, which, in essence, is deliberately constructing watermarks, or an entire cohesion. You might find it help-ful to think of your energy body as having primary and secondary programs to prioritize what you focus on.

Programs, themselves, are priorities, or degrees of com-mitment, whether conscious or not. Many of our actions are based on programs that we have not deliberately cre-ated, unconscious programs acquired without any thought—even though they can control our lives.

A Spirit-based program contains the full essence of your being. If it's your primary program, it's the basis of a cohesion that most closely connects you with the influences of Spirit; that is, if your first priority is to live a life with Spirit. Your secondary programs are concerned with em-ployment, relationships, hobbies, and other activities. If they are of a path with heart, they support your primary program.

Say, for instance, that living a life with Spirit is your primary program. To support this, you groom a livelihood based on a path with heart, which is a secondary program. So you program yourself to find a job that makes you strong and happy. But the primary program might influence your thoughts about what is suitable employment. Following the directives of Spirit, you might take a job contrary to the image you have of yourself. This happened to me years ago when I first began working in bookstores. Taking those jobs made little sense to me at the time, but led to a successful career in the publishing industry.

For another example, say you have a primary program of healthy living and a secondary program of socializing. In other words, the healthy-living program is more impor-tant to you than the company of others. As a result, there may be times when your primary program intervenes and pulls you away from certain groups. Perhaps, unknown to you, people you're beginning to hang out with practice knife-cutting rituals. But something always happens—a friend keeps asking for help, you get more work to take home than usual, or you always have feelings to do something else—keeping you away from the group. In other words, the cohesion with greater power supersedes what the secondary program is trying to manifest.

So don't curse the unexpected. It may keep things interesting. It may save you trouble. It may save your life.

Purpose. One of don Juan's female apprentices, la Gorda, says that the key for a ranger to be an impeccable tracker is purpose. Her purpose was to enter the other world (*Second Ring*, 223–224).

Purpose is a combination of focusing toward, and flowing with, energies associated with a goal. It is an expression of your innermost wishes and thereby connects you intimately with the world. As with focus, if you shut down the flow of energy, you lose sense of your quest. If you turn open the nozzle too far, you squander your resources.

To sense this flow:

1. Remain in touch with the wellspring of energy, the core from which your purpose emanates.
2. Let it saturate your awareness as you let it gently rush forth into the world.
3. Feel it connect with your goal. Cultivate the feeling that your goal is already with you, alive and well.
4. Remain nonattached to the outcome, or to the conditions under which your purpose becomes realized. Accept your fate.

Thinking. Thought is a directive force. It has shaped civilization, and is extremely powerful. But it's also just one of many options.

It's currently in vogue to say "Thought manifests reality." Well, this is true . . . to an extent. Thought builds conditional energy fields. From these, we create and experience realities. Once you begin tapping intent, however, this "law of manifesting" falls short, way short of describing a complex process.

The Toltec world is a new universe of thoughts, many of which form into feelings. Just as with any world, your feelings validate the very things you think about, but when you stop your internal dialogue, realities evaporate and feelings change. Then all your thinking goes kaplooey.

Therefore, the greater force of manifesting is working directly with cohesion. Thinking helps you with this—until you decide to leave it behind.

Visualization, or Imaging. For our purposes, visualization may be considered a form of dreaming. Dreaming speeds up learning as you work more closely, more directly, with cohesion. That is, dreaming lets you witness what you place into motion faster than you can in the physical world. So you can test and measure your steps easier. You just "run a program" by visualizing different scenarios, feeling if they make sense, making adjustments, running the program again, then letting your body adjust to that energy. Your body knowledge then helps you reconstruct the program in your outer world, and thereby manifest it.

By using visualization and feeling together, you can get a handle on intent. "Intent is beckoned with the eyes," says don Juan (*Silence,* 144). For instance, use your imagination to connect with the first chakra. To help you, use red as a focus. Then feel that energy. Now imagine orange. Feel it. Work your way up through the chakras, then back. As you do, feel the movement of energy with your entire body. You're now learning to manage cohesion.

In psychological experiments, athletes who used visualization improved their abilities at rates higher than those who only practiced. They used their imagination to refine their "athlete" cohesion, which translated into better performance in the physical world. Some studies included the use of hypnosis, which might be a form of programming, and found the subjects learned how to relax and concentrate better.[1]

Furthermore, you reinforce your image of yourself throughout the day by what kinds of images you create. Notice how you think, feel, and visualize yourself at various times of the day. These imaging sessions occur in a split second. But over time they build a self-profile within your energy body. This, in turn, aligns you with that image of yourself, which then manifests that result. This applies to your health, your monetary prosperity, how you drive, and how you talk; in short, all facets of your life.

You may also use imagination to open up to potential. Pick a far-fetched goal. Say you want to build a flying saucer. Tap that energy, play with it, imagine it. Track it. Let it stretch your thoughts and feelings into new worlds.

Waiting. As a discipline, waiting is also force. It automatically provides focus, removes obstacles within your cohesion, establishes an energy line to the goal, and thereby aligns perception with the emanation of your goal. It allows all the shifts in watermarks and cohesion to fall into place. When they have, you've manifested what you were waiting for. Thus, you don't have to search for something; you can let it come to you. By shifting cohesion, you produce the intended results.

Patience, the principal element of waiting, is obtained by forging your path with heart. When you have built your world from the stance of a ranger, you've acquired patience. Combined with purpose and losing self-importance, you've gained balance.

Here's a waiting drill don Juan offers: A ranger knows that he is waiting, and what he is waiting for. While she waits, she laughs and enjoys herself.

A ranger waits for his or her *will*. People such as don Juan wait for freedom (*Separate*, 178; *Fire*, 121).

Will. *Will* is the active force of shifting cohesion. It gives you command over your cornerstones and chakras. As a result, it gives you command over your complete energy body. For example, whereas the heart chakra is the balance point of the physical body (it is the fourth among seven), *will* is the balance point of the energy body as a whole. As a result, by shifting your cohesion, you can manifest your heart's delight. However, doing so may turn the tide of freedom against you. So we'll touch base on the use and abuse of power in the next chapter.

It seems *will* has plenty of interesting and nontoxic uses, however. When don Genaro, a friend of don Juan's, for example, climbed a dangerous waterfall, he used his *will*. In doing so, he gave Castaneda a lesson in how to control it and the abilities it rendered. Don Juan prevented Castaneda's car from starting, he used his *will* on the car's "key joint," by preventing the spark plugs from igniting. In a grander maneuver, don Juan says that Toltecs tune their *wills* by playing with death, by stretching out into the unknown, and then letting their *wills* reassemble their bodies (*Separate,* 132, 240, 239).

In general, by intending yourself to develop your *will*, you gradually bring it to life. So throughout the day, bring yourself back to this point of reference. Learn to isolate the differences between perceiving the world through reason and through *will*. You may do so simply by establishing the intent, then paying attention. Doing so continually grooms your body knowledge. This, in turn, awakens *will*.

Furthermore, *will* provides a powerful perspective illustrating the essence of manifesting. Simply, manifesting is applying your total energy to what you want, then simultaneously getting out of your way to allow the possibility, and actuality, of something more appropriate or even greater than your wishes to occur.

Tips. A few odds and ends, and reminders:

1. Manifest from the moment, from the here and now. If you want your world to manifest in the future, you keep it there and away from you.
2. Be aware of opposite effects. If you try to keep your lover from slipping away from you, you'll cling. That will most likely drive the person away. If the person was leaving anyway, let go gracefully.
3. Don't leave something to chance. Do everything you can to fulfill your purpose.
4. Focus toward, but don't fixate on, your goal.
5. Remember that optimism is a sign of emotional intelligence, and an indication of those who achieve success. It is the lubricant that helps energies shift, thus making it easier to build a "success" cohesion.
6. Each decision adds to, or subtracts from, your cohesion and your quest.
7. Don't have cross purposes. Align your primary and secondary programs to work in support of each other.
8. Tension in your body often reflects work you're doing to create a new cohesion, and manifest a new life. The realignment to new emanations is work, so your body feels it. It's body knowledge at work.

Prosperity

Your sense of prosperity depends on how, what, and where you invest, not to mention what the results are. For example, if your goal is to acquire money, and you're investing loads of time and energy going after it, then you don't have what you think is an adequate amount, you feel less than prosperous.

Watching our bank accounts grow is a popular form of active-meditation. Break out the checkbook and gaze at those numbers! We'll even give up time with the spouse and kids if we get reinforced enough, if we realize the potential of more money. But there are other than financial forms of prosperity that can uplift our lives just as much—and often more. Don Juan, for instance, says that one of the most exciting things to do is to discover more about the emanations; specifically, through *seeing* (*Fire,* 164). In effect, he is saying we can become more prosperous by investing in our own resources; to open up to a grander vision than that of material gain. Expanding through the energy body expands your options.

Money is a cohesion. It is a pattern of energy. You can accent it and live for it, or you can relate to it in terms that promote your fuller evolution. If your goal is solely material wealth, you need to become flush with this energy for success. By doing so, you've evolved that portion of yourself. But at what cost? Possibly, your greater evolution.

This doesn't mean if you're financially successful you're doomed. It means your relationship with money ought to emanate from your greater path. If financial wealth is truly part of your path, good for you. If it's not, don't brood over it. We can all find an amazing amount of prosperity with or without money. We can cultivate prosperity of Spirit. We can feel like a million bucks. We can feel like the entire world is ours by becoming the entire world. Don Juan says the effect of *seeing* is that a person "becomes everything by becoming nothing" (*Separate,* 186). From one angle, it's because *seeing* helps you cut through the layers of self-importance, of defining and reflecting about the world. Doing so helps you find your natural place in the world, your path with heart.

I've found that a path with heart contains the energy for a livelihood. Indeed, the title of Marsha Sinetar's popular book *Do What You Love, the Money Will Follow* captures the essence of this.[2] In addition, the Buddhist equivalent of developing a path with heart involves adhering to *The Eight-fold Path*, including *right conduct*, *right intent*, and *right livelihood*, which seems like the Buddhist reflection of being a ranger. In short, then, right livelihood is a devotion. It is a way to remain firmly on your path while earning a living.[3]

In general terms, if you have your path, you have yourself. As a result, you're not in the cohesion of "want" or "need," which means you're prosperous. You've therefore manifested prosperity in the fullest sense of the word.

$$\mathscr{D}\ \mathscr{D}\ \mathscr{D}$$

Layers upon layers of energy currents—winds of energy from this dimension and others—influence our world, our lives. I also believe that there are ways to hook into and sail these currents. This chapter has been a tour of the nuts and bolts of your sailing vessel. In broad strokes, the Toltec Way is about the art and craft of navigation. The next section presents core features of the Toltec system and how to apply them to your life.

PART IV

A
TOLTEC
QUEST
OF
EVOLUTION

8

IT HELPS TO HAVE A CEMENT TRUCK

All metaphysical paths that have withstood the test of time across centuries have common elements. They have theory, or worldview, for instance, to order your thoughts and guide your steps, and a discipline with techniques to bring the theory to life. The very best systems incorporate these into a staging ground to launch perception into regions beyond their own views. This makes them evolutionary.

Earlier I mentioned that this book is intended as a reference for those who are traveling a metaphysical path. There's no doubt, however, that the foundation of *Tracking Freedom* has been poured from the cement truck of the Toltec Way. In this chapter, therefore, let's explore the Toltec system, its components and stages of growth. From this, you may find comparable elements in your path and then further crystallize your knowledge, your way of *being*.

Tracking and Dreaming

Tracking and dreaming are two major aspects of Toltec philosophy. They relate to types of energy as well as to types of people. Thus far, this book has mostly explored tracking. Tracking is energy of stability, of definition, of pattern, of controlled growth, and of the skills relating to these. Trackers tend to be practical, easygoing, and relate well with people.

Dreaming is energy of expansion, of natural wildness, of swift transformation, of raw power, and of the behaviors relating to these. Dreamers tend to be dreamy-eyed, feel like they're never home anywhere in the physical world, strain the resources of those with whom they come into contact, bounce freely from one energy to another, and act like they're not grounded in what's going on about them (quite often, they're not).

Toltecs groom both of these energies. You can, for instance, tap dreaming to boost your level of tracking. I frequently enter dreaming to establish the logic or pattern of my books. I just place myself in the energy of what I'm writing about, then let the dreaming energies go to work and reveal what's on the agenda. I either *see* what is to be written, or come out of dreaming with a sense of several new paragraphs.

In turn, you can make greater headway in dreaming by becoming a better tracker. Proceeding to a new dreaming level requires that you have a degree of control over the previous level. The tracking skills of being grounded and centered, remaining inaccessible, and having stability of purpose, all provide a constancy that carries over into dreaming. Dreaming pulls you into your energy body, tracking pushes you into it; dreaming explodes you into it, tracking ushers you into it. Each supports the other; in a leapfrog manner they expand your evolution.

In addition, tracking relates to the first energy field, and dreaming to the second field. By consolidating these energies, you bolster the entire energy body. By intending to reach freedom, you stand a chance of lighting up the entire energy body, experiencing "all that is human," then evolving beyond the human condition to pure awareness.

Trackers and Dreamers

Trackers and dreamers have different experiences of energy. Each personality connects with the world in different ways, and deploys or uses energy in different ways. As Emilito (a member of don Juan's team) says, whether in dreaming or in waking, trackers plan then carry out their plans. Dreamers, on the other hand, jump into any reality without regard for plans.[1] So that you may better acquaint yourself with these energies, the following tidbits compare and contrast them. Watch for both of these expressions in your behavior, then practice the basics of losing self-importance, using your death as an adviser, altering routines, and other skills to balance and refine each of them.

Trackers build cohesions step by step.
Dreamers enter new cohesions in one swoop.

Trackers purposefully consolidate energy.
Dreamers keep awareness open to radical transformation.

Trackers develop flexibility and fluency among different worlds.
Dreamers are often black-and-white, totally in a perspective or totally out of it. Literally.

Trackers tend to be lighthearted.
Dreamers often become morose and obsessed, seemingly lost within the energies of their world.

Trackers find knowledge through shifting social identities.
Dreamers find knowledge through shifting the various dreams of reality.

Trackers find meaning in stability, then hook dreaming into the physical and build from there.

Dreamers take their awareness, fixate on it, then project that onto others.

Trackers have a difficult time accessing the full robustness of dreaming.

Dreamers have a difficult time relating to what they consider limitations of the physical world, and the requirements of building something over time.

Trackers isolate components of a problem, then apply strategic pressure to open doors.

Dreamers sense options, then open doors.

Trackers need training in dreaming to stretch into the energy body.

Dreamers need training in tracking to get down to earth.

If trackers don't commit to dreaming, they get lost in the nuances of their wondrous accomplishments.

If dreamers don't commit to tracking, they get lost in the currents of their own dreams.

In both instances, it's a matter of getting lost in self-importance.

If it seems that I am slightly kinder to trackers in this portrayal, it is because you're relating these features to the social base, to what has meaning in the world of people. A dreamer wouldn't give a fig for all this chatter about what a dreamer is like. A tracker would assess it under his or her own terms. The Toltec social base of values is different from what is normally found. I also may have given a slight edge to trackers because I have found that tracking is essential. Without it, time and time again, I have seen people squander their potential for realization, as they lose themselves in the mysteries of dreaming states that have no purpose. Having a clear head and heart is required for this journey. Tracking and dreaming are professional skills. They require ongoing development. Getting lost in a dream occurs more frequently than we realize.

Stages of Personal Evolution

The Toltec Way outlines definite stages of evolution. Each stage of transformation is a new cohesion, with a new set of watermarks, and a new relationship with the world. The length of time it takes to bring a stage to life depends on the person. It might take one person fifteen years to become a ranger, another only three years. If you're truly on the path, such distinctions don't carry much weight. If you're putting your all into the work, that sense of balance is enough to carry you forward. To some degree, the notion that "the journey matters more than the destination" is true. Even so, arriving successfully at a destination is a great thing to experience.

Each stage of evolution reflects growing into the moment. The more you plug in to potential, the more you're aware of yourself and the world. The more sense you have, the more you can *be* in the moment.

At each stage you must claim your knowledge. You need to have experience to develop skills to acquire more experience, and you need to have the wherewithal to make sense of your experience. You also need to claim knowledge in such a way that you remain open to even more experience. To claim knowledge, it must become a matter of body knowledge. Therefore, approach your lessons from multiple angles. Relate to body knowledge from each of the chakra energies, for instance. Or, if you talk with an elemental spirit, how does the experience affect your physical world, your emotions, your thoughts, your spiritual values? Assess and integrate the experience. Change your thoughts, your feelings, your relation to the world as required. Make firm decisions on how you want to proceed.

Establish new watermarks. Build new cohesions. Then let go and flow as you challenge your world once again.

Your meanings in life, your values, and your interpretations change at each stage. If they don't, you haven't done much to transform yourself. Keep in mind that changing your cohesion changes the world. To take a crack at freedom, the idea is to shed all meaning, values, and interpretations that stem from worldviews. Your cohesion has to be pretty clean to do this. There's always a bunch of karma to burn off to get clean. As such, each stage also reflects having lost more self-importance.

To get to a point where you can experience the world without the ballast of a worldview is a piece of work, to say the least. When you stabilize a new cohesion, a new stage, you'll feel natural in that energy. Remember, though, that all conditional fields feel like home, feel natural . . . until they exhaust you from complacency. Building a true natural energy field reflects a magnificent, awe-inspiring freedom quest. It is a stage beyond stages. Don't settle for less.

The following is a general outline of the stages along a Toltec path to freedom. The *evolution* involves the dynamics of the specific stage. The *obstacle* is what don Juan refers to as a "natural enemy" (*Teachings,* 93).

The Apprentice

Evolution. Simply put, at this stage you learn how to work your butt off. Expect to drill yourself on a variety of seemingly nonsensical exercises. Don't expect to make any gains. Expect to be exposed to some wild ideas about the world. Don't expect to understand anything.

But remember: From the perspective of a natural energy field, at each stage we're all beginners. The Zen mind *is* the beginner's mind: open, clear, yielding, strong.

Obstacle: Fear. Fear is the inability to shift cohesion. This means behavior is rigid and thinking is fundamentalist. Initially, the physical body translates this lack of suppleness as fear. Later, it is felt as a lack of momentum. In fighting fear, you gain new experiences as you act in unfamiliar ways. The more experience you have, the more you bring your energy body to life. This results in having more energy, more personal power, and therefore more momentum.

Don Juan says the way to fight fear is simple: each and every time you find yourself at a crossroad, and you determine that the only thing keeping you from proceeding in a certain direction is fear, then you head in that direction—even if your fear seems insurmountable. To turn back is to be defeated. Don Juan says a defeated person may turn into a bully or just remain scared until his dying day (*Teachings*, 95).

The Ranger

Evolution. At this stage, it's important to keep doing what you've been doing. Practice and refine your basic tracking skills. But you've also elevated your level of skill. Like getting a new belt in martial arts training, you're getting better. Just don't look for an outward symbol. You're not going to get sergeant's stripes, a new color of belt, or a sorority pin. By now, however, you do have a handle on your path. You can apply your knowledge. You can deliberately (albeit modestly) shift your cohesion into different tracking and dreaming states. In a nutshell, you know what you want from life, and how to get it (*Teachings*, 96).

You've also committed to this path. It's part of your natural evolution; it's part of your path with heart. By developing this awareness, you've learned to wait. Having learned patience, nonattachment, responsibility, and the power of making decisions in the light of your death, you've become a ranger (*Separate,* 184). As this is the core discipline of the Toltec path, features of what it means to be a ranger are further outlined in the next chapter.

Obstacle: Clarity. "Lost within a vision" is a good way to characterize the negative effect of clarity. Oddly enough, becoming clear is an obstacle as well as a step. While you've enhanced your perception and thus gained a clearer view of the world, the work you've done on your energy body leads you to conclude that you've figured it all out. After all, from your apprenticeship you learned how to build your life, which means you've built a foundation of strong cohesion, which means you can see clearly. From the perspective of further evolution, however, you've learned enough to know just a little. Some patterns you now perceive will unfold just as you *see* them, others won't. Sometimes you're just getting ahead of yourself. Other times the patterns belong to another dimension, an alternate reality, as it were. This is frustrating, especially since you've paid a pretty hefty price to get here, and now you have to start anew. But here's why it's important to continue practicing your basic skills.

Clarity means you've gained momentum. As a result, you're changing the direction of your life. It doesn't mean you know how to handle your new relationship with the world. This is why don Juan advises treating clarity as though it might be a mistake, to defy clarity as you defied fear. Exercise patience. Make your decisions carefully (*Teachings,* 97).

One suggestion is to continue working with fear. By now you know that fear is inertia, a reluctance to change direction. You might also consider it a lack of suppleness within the energy body that keeps your cohesion fixed. When you have a sensation resembling fear, track it. Find out its origin. Maybe you need a refresher in bouncing over the fear obstacle. Maybe you're learning the tensions surrounding your cohesion. In any case, you're working with the properties of energy rather than with the ordinary considerations of what fear once meant. Keep building momentum, which is the same thing as saying keep building your personal power. Fighting fear does this. So keep up the good fight.

To be defeated by clarity (or by any obstacle) means you've given up. You've hit the wall of a new level and have accepted the status quo. The wind has gone from your sails. Your tires are flat. If you don't overcome clarity, you'll stay on the surface of knowledge, or perhaps you'll become a clown as you go about telling others how much you know (*Teachings,* 96).

Let's take a practical business situation to look at the effects of clarity. Say you've been struggling tooth and nail to make your business go. You've built a reputation for service, quality, and dedication. Then, after years of toil, you hit pay dirt. You've got a product that everyone is asking for. Revenues soar. You've shifted to a new level. You've crossed the first obstacle to business success.

Like many businesses in this situation, you take your money and invest it in everything you've always wanted. More employees, better equipment, software upgrades. Your vision is finally coming to pass. You're *clear.* But wait. You've overextended yourself. You're missing a beat during the expansion, and are no longer delivering your products in the timely manner your customers have grown accustomed to—and for which they have given you their respect (not to mention their money). As a result, you're losing your business power (i.e., personal power) to your thoughts and feelings about the way you want it all to be. You're no longer managing your resources efficiently and with prudence. You've fumbled away the connection between your visionary goals and the business practicalities. Your customers are now grumbling, almost begrudging your success. Having worked for many companies, I've seen this dynamic on more than one occasion.

The remedy is to go back to the basics that enabled you to deliver quality and service in the first place. Return to your prior stage of growth to extract its wisdom. Relearn frugality. Remember not to overextend your grasp recklessly while pushing yourself beyond your limits. It's an interesting dance, knowing when to move and when to wait. This, in essence, is the dance of clarity. From this dance, you learn balance. You learn how to handle momentum, the movement of energy, the movement of your personal energy through these things we call time and space.

Your perceptions resulting from clarity stem from potential. They are the glimmerings of freedom. They are dreams. They are illusions. They may or may not be different from actuality, from what may be realizable. It'll take years of more work to figure out the difference.

Clarity also has an effect on physical perception. That is, you begin to view the world as two-dimensional. Depth, the third dimension, is only a sense of the world. Yet images are sharper, clearer, and colors are more vivid. The more you work with your clarity, the more you begin to figure out how the bubble of perception works. You *see* your internal and external worlds merge, so that they do not have the same meaning as they once did. Each reflects the other. You gain a knowledge of intent that allows you to grasp how manifesting truly occurs: by controlling your internal cohesion, you shape your external world. By hooking on to the energy in your external world, you shape your internal cohesion. Having this awareness means you're just about ready to step into the world of the Toltec.

The Toltec

Evolution. As a ranger, you've learned to wait for your *will*. Don Juan says that all people are connected with the world through *will*, through the luminous fibers centered in the abdomen (*Separate*, 33). For most people, however, *will* is dormant. The hallmark of the Toltec stage, therefore, is the activation of *will*. Throughout your journey to freedom you have in some way witnessed its expression and felt its power. Now it's alive and well. As a result, you have command over your cohesion. In doing so, you have completed building a nonordinary conditional energy field. You are a full-blown practitioner of Toltec knowledge.

During this journey of growing *will*, don Juan says a person performs impossible tasks, or impossible things just happen. He also says the person will most likely experience growing pains; yep, real pain, including convulsions (now there's something to look forward to). Indeed, he says the more pain a person experiences, the stronger will be his or her *will*. Don Juan continues, saying that when the convulsions end, the person can connect with and touch anything "with a feeling that comes out of his body" from a spot near the navel. This feeling, he says, is *will* (*Separate*, 185, 33).

A useful exercise for learning more about *will* is to observe whether you're perceiving the world with your reason or your body. When you're using reason, the world is distant, seemingly objective, and is upheld by your thoughts *about* the world. When you use your body, you feel connected, sense your relationship, and have a knowing beyond thoughts that you're part of the world. This is body knowledge.

Obstacle: Power. Having command over your cohesion means you can determine the events in your life. It's all in the play of the bubble. It's all a matter of focusing those mirrors to reflect whatever you want. Proceed in a narcissistic manner, however, and you're doomed.

Relating this to the prior business example, having power means you can dominate. You can determine how other companies do business through the way you operate. A large distributor, for instance, can determine how a small production company must schedule shipments, file paperwork, and manage other resources. In some measure, for good or ill, the distributor is calling the shots.

On a personal level, power means you can literally create your own reality, and do so masterfully. Having control of your *will* means you have control of your cohesion. As you change your cohesion, you change your external world. You can have anything you want merely by aligning yourself with that energy. If you give in to power, though, don Juan says you'll never learn to manage your resources. You'll never claim the fullness of your birthright. You'll stay lost in a sea of desire (*Teaching,* 97).

The way to manage power is the same as with the other obstacles: don't use it. With fear, you learned to generate momentum, to move energy. With clarity, you learned to temper and restrain your energy. With power, you learn how to manage your complete energy body.

However, don Juan advises that there does come a time when you have all of your resources in balance. It is then, and only then, that you know when and how to use power. Such wisdom is gained only after a lifetime struggle, a lifetime of questing for freedom. At this stage, you exit conditional energy fields and enter the domain of a natural field. You've become a person of knowledge (*Teachings,* 98).

The Person of Knowledge

Evolution. Don Juan says that while a Toltec may have a very strong *will*, it is possible that the person does not *see*. He indicates that this means only a person of knowledge perceives the world "with his senses and with his *will* and also with his *seeing*." (*Separate,* 181). *Seeing*, remember, is the force of perception that splits energy away from conditional fields. It is a direct connection with the world, unencumbered by reason. It doesn't need a platform of conditions for it to deliver meaningful awareness. Therefore, it removes you from the necessity of using metaphysical structures to bolster your quest. You're becoming free.

Until now you've been in conditional fields. Your world has been fraught with projection; a world built from self-importance. At this stage, though, you have the knowledge to break free, and rest within the embrace of all creation. Like a drop of water in the ocean, your energy body is fully connected with the Eagle's emanations. Hence, there's little projection. The mirrors of the bubble of perception have become so thoroughly transparent that "inner" and "outer" cease to exist. From having tempered your first energy field, your sense of order neatly meshes with the expansive energies of the second field. You're on cruise control, living life simply to be living it. As don Juan says, a person of knowledge has shed honor, dignity, family, name, and country, and has "only life to be lived" (*Separate,* 107). You are now *being.* You have fully integrated the discipline forged from the long haul to maintain this unparalleled state of awareness.

Obstacle: Old age. The energy you've peaked for a lifetime begins to wear thin. Put another way, the energy you've built is getting harder to keep on track. You're old now, and you're getting tired.

Push this energy away! If you lose yourself in your tiredness, your energy will warp and reduce you to feebleness. Live your fate through, says don Juan, and you'll experience a rare delicacy. In what sounds like a pure mystical experience, he says the energies of clarity, power, and knowledge combine to produce an exquisite state of awareness that makes the entire journey worthwhile (*Teachings,* 99).

The Seer

Evolution. Don Juan says that *seeing* is the final accomplishment of a person of knowledge (*Journey,* 233). In this sense, I believe he means mastering the ability to manage energies of cosmic proportion. It seems as though it takes that much training not to get lost in *seeing*. Evidently, the old cycle of Toltec seers, who were considered masters in handling the energy body, became very fixated and obsessive about their *seeing*—so much so that they lost their nonattachment, dove back into fear, and became piously reverent—a terrible predicament for a Toltec (*Fire*, 18).

It is also my sense (and my rendering of Toltec teachings) that by the time don Juan had trained Castaneda, he burned away his karmic connection with Castaneda as he burned with the Fire from Within. Then, by the time he returned to take others under his wing (yet another karma), he had become a complete seer, a consummate practitioner at managing energy. He was able to step in and out of dimensions—including to and from the third energy field—at *will*. I can only speculate about what passion and mysteries he must be experiencing. Perhaps his energy ripples through creation, continuously expanding beyond worlds that are themselves only at the edge of imagination. Beyond this inkling, I have not a clue.

What I *see* now was quite beyond my imagination twenty years ago; to make a couple more leaps of perception and place myself in his steps stops imagination dead in its tracks—almost.

The Fire of Freedom

This is a special version of what Castaneda calls the *Fire from Within*. It consists of stimulating and bringing to life the entire energy body. At a certain point, the physical body evaporates from the physical world and completely enters another energy field. The old cycle of Toltecs fired off their energy bodies into the second field, possibly getting trapped for eternity (*Fire,* ch. 15). Keep in mind that the first and second energy fields comprise the Toltec definition of what it means to be human. And this definition is pretty far-reaching. Shapeshifting into plants and animals, for instance, was all part of a day's work for old-cycle Toltecs (*Dreaming,* 78). As a result, they were keeping themselves pinned within specific areas of the energy body. As grand as their accomplishments were, they remained locked within a certain domain.

The new cycle of Toltecs, of which I consider don Juan to be a shining example, gives the quest a different spin, that of pure freedom. This means evolving beyond the entire human condition into the third energy field; a radical transformation, a true evolution. This version of the Fire from Within is what I call the Fire of Freedom.

The idea is to become the essence of all that is human, retain this knowledge, then jump out of the human domain (*Dreaming,* 73). In her book *Being-in-Dreaming,* Florinda Donner points out that a person needs a well-developed reason to make this leap, as it helps you avoid excesses.[2] Rather than lose oneself in shapeshifting, for example, the logic of the path dictates that staying on track for even greater accomplishments is a higher priority. Shapeshifting may facilitate exploring the energy body, but is not the be-all and end-all.

Eligio, another of don Juan's apprentices, burned with the Fire because he knew how to let go (*Second Ring,* 46). He entirely accepted his fate. He blended with the world. He stopped the world. So he was able to leave it. As a result, he gained the freedom to be human or to be whatever form of consciousness he experiences in other energy fields. However, discernments should be made as to whether these feats are of the Fire from Within, or the Fire of Freedom—your call.

Evolution of the Toltec Way

The Toltec Way has spawned many lineages, many energy lines. Don Juan says he is part of a specific line dating back to 1723. This is when the nagual Sebastian reclaimed many lost Toltec practices (*Fire,* ch. 15). This is also the beginning of the new cycle. With Sebastian's discoveries, Toltecs had even more experience with which to compare and contrast. As a result, they were able to foster an understanding of personal evolution. Although the old cycle was locked up in a prison of its own doings, it also served as a bridge. Without the efforts, explorations, and examinations of its practitioners, we would not have such a rich philosophy today. While the old cycle lost itself in sorcery, it led to the new cycle's interest in freedom.

Modern Toltecs examine the world from the premise that it is made up of energy. This includes studying the dynamics of emanations, different dimensions of reality, other forms of organic and inorganic life, and the human energy body. The procedures to do this separate one metaphysical path from another. Toltecs, for instance, use death as an adviser, perform the gait of power, work to remain inaccessible, divvy up energies between tracking and dreaming, and use a theoretical structure of three energy fields. Zen Buddhists, on the other hand, often strive to stay away from power plays such as the gait of power and dreaming. They do, however, accentuate basic exercises for nonattachment, inaccessibility, and losing self-importance.

A remarkable example of Toltec studies, Castaneda's books provide a common reference to don Juan's teachings; that is, to modern Toltec teachings. As more people follow a Toltec path, various sects will most likely sprout. Just as Buddhism and Christianity have sects, there will be groups of like-minded people who get to a certain stage and put their own spin on the Toltec system. They will define particular options and will want to follow those options. For example, one group might *see* chakras as part of the human energy band, while another group *sees* it differently. One group might be more traditional, and another group more avant garde.

As these tributaries form from the greater river, there will be costs and benefits. One cost is that the Toltec system will become bureaucratic, organized, and strictly consensual. Remember, this is what don Juan warned us of when he advised against becoming "official sorcerers in residence." To become part of a status quo automatically removes awareness from the flow of evolution as perception becomes locked in a conditional field. This will happen because this is what humans do, or at least have done time and time again. People want to know, and ordinary knowing is having a fixed foundation of knowledge. To think that there really is no fixed knowledge is not rational. By all means, we must be rational . . . even if it means harming, in thought or flesh, our neighbors. Right, I mean harm the ones who don't agree with our reasonableness.

Then, too, some people may not feel compelled to journey completely to freedom. Some might find value with just developing their path with heart. So compared with those aiming for third-field freedom, this group might seem tame. But if the overall path helps someone, then that's great. It's like the pioneers who picked up stakes with the intention of traveling to California, only to settle down in Kansas. These people also possessed courage, and, anyway, I hear that's where the Wizard of Oz lives.

One benefit of managing a variety of views is that people learn that their views are just that, views. So if folks don't start thinking theirs is *the* right view, then perhaps we'll all realize that different groups are all expressions of Spirit. All denominations should recognize the value of other paths, and partake in that value, while steadfastly awakening their own nature. Remember when a person lashes out against others, it is projection in motion. And haven't we figured out that the world holds infinite potential? Holds possibilities beyond projection?

Then there are the Toltecs who will bring forward yet another new cycle. This will be done not by their intent, but by Spirit working through them. By ruthless adherence to discipline and strategy, they will allow the force of Spirit to call forth another dawn, a new and masterful expression of the Toltec Way.

Hi Ho, Silver!

9

LAUNCH
PAD
101

Any path is neither better nor worse than any other, save for the quality of life it provides. Whether you pick up garbage or serve as the president of a country, the measurements for success are the same. How well do you live your life? How much good feeling do you have? How much peace do you have? How rich in Spirit are you? These things are measurements of quality, and of a path with heart.

Quality is enhanced when it comes from being more deeply connected with the universe, and becoming more a part of the essence of life, rather than just getting turned on to a more limited high—career or otherwise. A path with heart, a mainstay of Toltec teachings, plugs you directly into the world. It delivers a current of energy that sustains—indeed, nourishes—your life. It also reflects the beginning of knowing how to manage your karma, and therefore manage your cohesion.

Having cultivated a path with heart is the beginning of Toltec advanced study and practice, if there even is such a thing as "advanced." If you take a college course, "Psychology 101" for instance, you're at the beginning of university level, or advanced, study. Yet there are many levels of university studies that advance learning. It usually takes a lot of preparation to get to the doorstep of any of them. Hence, "advanced" is relative to the task at hand. In addition, if the evolutionary ladder is infinite, then there is no above or below, no ahead of or behind. There simply *is*.

Consider also that we're not talking just about personal growth. We're not trying to find our way just a little bit better than before. We're dealing with evolution, with completely new levels of expansion and transformation.

Traveling a path with heart is matching your energy body with the Eagle's emanations, those of "human" as well as those of "you." By doing so, you find your natural place in the world. By becoming more natural, you wake up to more of the world about you. On the flip side, to find your path you have to become more aware. You have to wake up to your sense of the natural order. This increased motion sets energy in motion to continue your awakening, transforming the way you look at, *see*, and interact with the world. This transformation is your evolution.

To recap the stages of growth, the power of this path elevates you into clarity, with the costs and benefits of that stage and obstacle. So don't let your clarity make you believe your experiences represent a universal scheme of things. A path with heart is also a path with power. It brings your life into focus, thus bringing your world into focus. You become more aware, and thus more capable. Keep in mind that what you discover may not necessarily be the way it is for everyone, just the way it is for you. Therefore, abide by your discipline and pretend your knowledge is almost a mistake, and continue confronting your fears—at least what seem to be your fears. Remember that fear is a lack of flow—a lack of suppleness—in your energy body. Continue working on positive attitudes, and on nonpatterning in general. There comes a time when your clarity has stabilized and you're dealing with real power. Again, to handle power, continue your discipline of letting the world be as it is, not as you want it to be. At the same time, take charge of your life as you deliberately enter the world of Spirit. As a result, you'll develop an intimate relationship with the world.

Forging a path creates a conscious connection with Spirit. It's the tree trunk through which sap rises, and from which limbs grow. Connecting your limbs with the world about you strengthens the trunk and generates more branches; that is, by extending your energy into previously unused emanations, you temper your energy body, thereby bringing more of it to life.

Each stage of growth is principally a matter of losing more self-importance. Because you're telling yourself less about how the world is, as you lose self-importance you automatically make more of a connection with the emanations. As this occurs, you become the emanations. Actually, you always were a part of them. You just forgot. Anyway, when you stabilize this complete energetic realization, you're in the domain of a person of knowledge. You're such a part of cosmic nature that you can step off the foundation that once stabilized your growth. You can leave the path and rest easy that you'll continue to grow in bounding leaps.

A path is a form of karma. You find your *predilections* (your innate, or natural, characteristics) by opening up to your natural path. Say one of your predilections is to draw. By working with that energy, and purposefully becoming better at it, you awaken a portion of the energy body, the "drawing" cohesion. By working with a variety of predilections, you awaken several cohesions. Hooking them together—relating each to the others—forges a path that brings greater potentials within you to life, to realization. A path with heart, therefore, is a path of freedom.

The karma of it is that by isolating energies that had been waiting to come to life—your predilections—you establish a tension of growth that burns off barnacles that collected from misusing, or from not using, your energy body's resources. Since this form of karma awakens you, you begin traveling deeper to your core. As you do, you become more and more intimate with the world. You gain the freedom to jettison everything you don't need because you have loads of meaning in your life. Before establishing a freedom path, many of us grab on to anything. Sex, drugs, and rock-'n'-roll become mainstays of living, just so that we'll have some sense of relation to the world. Just so we'll *feel* something, anything. By using our resources in a helter-skelter manner, however, we squander our intelligence.

Now remember, getting rid of everything unnecessary is one of Florinda's tracking principles (*Gift,* 281). This lets you free up energy for other applications. It makes you more fluid, more adaptable, more independent, more open, and more able to shift cohesion; in short, more intelligent. The combined effect of all of this is that you gain enough energy to tailor and direct all the elements of your life to help you reach your goals: quintessential tracking. Dreamers do the same, but in a different way. Don Juan says that dreamers mold their lives to fit their specifications (*Dreaming,* 33). Tracking and dreaming, then, are different forms of intentionality. Strategize and build for trackers; sense and feel a new dream for dreamers. The result is the same: a natural path. But first you have to know that the option to tailor your life exists.

Predilections

Predilections are God-given traits, Eagle-given traits if you relate them to Toltec philosophy. They are what make up *you*, at least the "you" you experience while traveling this world. They are songs from your core, beckoning you to wake up to a fuller life. Put them all together and you have a force pulling you into action, and into *being*.

The natural self is a mystery. Unraveling this mystery is where predilections and a path with heart come in. Think of your energy body as a particle of energy. It turns out that this particle is dormant, like a sheet of music is dormant, waiting to be played, waiting to express the energy it holds, waiting to come to life. Just as different songs have different titles, themes, and notes, each particle is unique. Now then, each predilection represents a single cord, a strand of energy, inside the particle. Pluck at it and you generate sound. If you learn to play it, you get music. The better you play, the more harmonious the results. Orchestrate enough cords and you get a complete song, as well as the toe-tapping time of your life.

Predilections also serve to filter the immense amount of energy we're immersed in. If we didn't have them, we'd probably explode from an infusion of energy. Thus they act as *shields*. This shielding effect has a high and a low side. The high side is that it gives you a world to relate to, an intimate portrayal of humanness. You gain ideas and behaviors that carry meaning. Whether you end up a stockbroker or a telephone repairperson, your path sets you firmly on the earth. You've tailored your life to find your niche, and your shields offer protection from energy overload. The low side is that as you tailor your life, you reduce your options. Reduce them enough and you lock away your awareness. Give them too much emphasis and your shields become barriers. Indeed, don Juan says that as we grow older we exhaust only the world of normal human options. The things that people do are only shields, he says, not the substance of the world. So as we focus too much on them, they confine our options and wreck our lives. For a ranger, this is too high a price to pay (*Separate*, 260–265).

The idea, therefore, is to generate strength and peace of mind without losing flexibility. This, combined with a ruthless quest to push past all barriers of perception, is the nonpatterning of predilections. These energies come into awareness from the silence within. They are expressed outwardly to provide stability of purpose. When you've broken through into new territory, these energies offer a beacon to help you return and consolidate your gains. For instance, when you learn to play with your *will* and it expands into regions that offer no meaning, you need something to restore your senses. You don't want to stay in never-never land, but you do want to explore it. With time, energy, and experience you'll produce sense of your explorations. Therefore, for the times you stretch way out there, your predilections pull your *will* back into focus, thereby restoring meaning. But it will be a new focus because reconsolidating your *will* delivers new knowledge. Then you go at it again, and again, and again, until your *will* activates. By this time, you have intentionally developed a set of predilection shields, which translates to a path with heart.

In this light, predilections are the grand karma between you and the world. Lousy shields keep you on the defensive, reactionary to new thoughts and feelings. Shields that are part of a path with heart yield to mystery, and foster a sense of well-being.

Predilections are also watermarks. They are aspects of cohesion. In building the life of a ranger, there comes a time when you have to revamp your watermarks. You have to discover and bring to life a new set—yes, a completely new group—of predilections. Whereas you once might have had a tendency to sulk when you were in a situation you didn't understand, now you have to cultivate a predilection of wonder and openness. On a more personal level, for example, you might acknowledge your joy in writing. Where once you avoided it, now you own up to it. So you take a few classes, talk with other writers, practice with a variety of styles, and consciously develop that skill. You do so solely for the love of it. It is this type of predilection, the ones built on love, peace, strength, and joy (possibly with a mix of drama and humor), that are the shields of a ranger.

As a result, your new set of watermarks forges a strong yet resilient cohesion. You can then withstand the shock of entering a new world for the first time, or of talking with a different species of life. You'll also have the means to regain your bearings, fortify your integrity, and, in general, find your balance in this world when shocks throw you for a loop.

As you open yourself to the mystery of the universe, you'll become infused with more energy. Large infusions will naturally be too much for your current cohesion to handle. So you'll open up, get clobbered, close up, integrate the new energy and knowledge, then do it all over again. At first, it's quite difficult and very strenuous, this dance of evolution. Later on down the path, you'll love the adventure of it. You'll rejoice in waiting for the moment that you'll experience chunks of knowledge. This is what ranger predilections help provide. Read on for tips on how to discover them.

Building a Path with Heart

What are you doing in this thing called *life*? Are you flopping all over the place like a fish out of water every time someone says, "Boo"? Are you bullying your way through the world, stomping on everything so you can be right? Are you quietly building a career? How much responsibility have you taken on, how much personal responsibility have you assumed, and just how in charge of *your* life are you? These questions are for you, and you alone, to answer.

Each question relates to the path you travel, and how you're traveling it. Trying to figure out the right relationships among these and other issues could have you bouncing from path to path for a lifetime (not to mention bouncing off walls) and really not getting anywhere. Influenced by the excesses of old-cycle Toltecs, the new cycle studied and experimented to find a workable relationship between self and world. They did this so they could explore the outermost edges of human perception and not get lost; indeed, make their journeys usable for continued personal evolution as well as for humankind at large.

Don Juan, for example, provides a basic formula for brewing rangers: that of using death as an adviser, nonattachment, and deliberately selecting shields. From my own experience I know that this dynamic mix delivers you to patience. You automatically arrive at patience from being completely on a path with heart, which, according to don Juan, is what his magic potion is intended for (*Separate,* 183–184).

Be silent. Pay attention. These are your first ingredients. They may be the last, for that matter, if you're good at it. Get out of your own way and listen to the silent murmuring of Spirit living within you. Listen, observe, let go, use your body knowledge. Feel yourself blend naturally with the world. Spirit will guide you. Seems like all the bigwig teachers say that. Seems like it's true.

To track freedom, some things are certain: Building your life on social standing, on the pursuit of material wealth, on getting more people into bed only pulls you off the path. Now, you might be materially successful, but that doesn't mean your life is built on it. This is where your death comes in. If you're placing your life on the line, what will you die for? That guy across the street might be "to die for," but what do you want to spend the very essence of your life doing? What kind of a life do you want? If you're going to die real soon, what do you want to do right *now*?

Got it figured out? Then go do it.

While you're doing it, sprinkle some nonattachment in there. Let that simmer for a while. How do you feel? What did you learn? Did you really give up that attachment? Ready for a grander concoction? Okay, get very serious (without forgetting to laugh). What would you like—no, what would you *love*—to build? What activities would make you happier? Stronger? More peaceful? Okay, they're yours.

Simple. Not for most people. Seems like we have to break a huge amount of momentum hurling us into oblivion, keeping us asleep at the wheel, making us groggy for eternity. One antidote is don Juan's "grog for the living." It lets you rise from sleep, regain respect for your life, and deliberately aim your energies in the directions that feed your heart. Take a sip. You're ready to launch.

Tracking exercises, then, help focus your trajectory. Fighting fear, for example, refines your edge. It gives you the gumption to use your death as an adviser in the first place. Then you have petty tyrants to help you out.

Working with a petty tyrant brings a lot to the surface. The value of sticking with the turmoil is that it helps you crystallize your awareness on multiple levels. Emotions become mentally recognizable, for instance. As a result, you can talk about what's bothering you, and your conceptualizations give you more control over wild emotional states because you have a way to direct that energy. As a result, you feel more stable. A petty tyrant also provides pressure (sometimes boiling pressure) to help you figure out what does have meaning for you, thus accelerating your pace of learning.

You also have to know when one path ends and another begins. At times, there will be a natural evolution of graceful motion where the end of one path and the beginning of another are seamless. Other times, you'll hit white water and will feel jostled all over the place. Sometimes a path just runs out of steam. At yet other times you must very carefully and skillfully assess your life. The joyful transitions are easy enough. The heartbreaking ones will get you going, exciting your energy body. Then you must figure out how to manage this energy.

You can be one with a path and still feel like you're on a hot burner. When the going gets tough, pay attention to what you're experiencing and learning. You have direction; you know what you're building. So are your difficulties burning off karma to help you realize greater goals? Or are you only proving to no one in particular that you can withstand pain? Only you can make these determinations. Only you can enact your decisions. Spirit is there to help, however. In an upcoming chapter, "Guidance Systems," we'll look at a variety of ways to navigate your path. For now, let's look at the essence of Toltec training, the discipline of a ranger.

A Ranger's Calling

As we're talking about this wonderful thing called evolution, do you get the idea that you have to be demented to make a good go of it? From time to time, it sure seems like it would help, that's for sure. But in the midst of a battle with a petty tyrant, of confusion over which way to turn, of having your life's meaning stripped from you, there is a saving grace in living a certain lifestyle. Don Juan, for instance, says that a Toltec's life is more precarious, perhaps even more dangerous, than the average person's life. He might get lost in another world, or people will plot against her. What helps a Toltec live a better life, he says, is the strength found in being a ranger (*Separate*, 258).

As reflecting a stage of growth, a ranger has learned the essential ins and outs of the Toltec Way, and is firmly on a path with heart. The person then begins applying knowledge. Where *cohesion*, *body knowledge*, and *petty tyrant* were once foreign concepts, they are now part and parcel of a day's work. Getting to the point of understanding them is what has enabled the person to handle a variety of viewpoints, including views of complete realities. This, in turn, is what helps a person grow out of conditional fields. All of this is part of the discipline that enables a ranger to plug in to the flow of evolutionary energies.

I recently met an elemental spirit—The Keeper, I call him—in the woods near my home. To me, this entity, who happens to have male energy, embodies all that I hold sacred about ranger discipline. The Keeper is part of at least two dimensions, that of humans and that of the more subtle energies of nature. Perhaps he can pick and choose, step in and out of them at his discretion, I don't yet know.

He is a massive figure, weighing in at several hundred pounds—if he were human, that is, and had a physical body. I *see* his body, which is the color of earth and tree bark combined. We talk about the land he roams, the land he dearly loves. He watches out as best he can for the life in his territory, and wonders why humans are so distant, so unconnected, so estranged, from the earth that nourishes us. The terms kind, gentle, strong, peaceful, and fierce all accurately portray this creature.

When I'm walking through forests, I feel connected to him, and through him I experience an unusual, heightened sense of the land. I feel like a ranger, like a wizard in training. I feel like my world comes straight out of Middle Earth, the land that J.R.R. Tolkien gave birth to. More on elementals later, for now let the Keeper guide your imagination about what kind of life you could be living.

Moving on, we find that two principal supports in a ranger's life are patience and impeccability.

Patience. Patience is a silent force that forms cohesions. It is the posture of waiting, and waiting in such a way that you don't waste energy. Remember the little singsong waiting drill from chapter 7? "A ranger knows that he is waiting, and what he is waiting for. While she waits, she laughs and enjoys herself." In addition, since the ranger has a full life as a result of having built a path with heart, the ranger wants nothing. Indeed, don Juan says that not wanting anything is a ranger's finest attainment (*Tales,* 242). This doesn't mean you can't like something, or can't gather more knowledge. It means keeping your awareness clear and unfettered. It means you don't waste time and energy trying to be something, or have something. Each time you intend to be something, like a teacher, for instance, removes you from the energy taking you to complete potential. By defining yourself, you've realized something out of potential, but not potential itself. You've become the pioneer who ended the quest and settled down before he wanted to, settled in a land he didn't truly love.

Patience is measured with the body, and is therefore a step toward managing body knowledge. Your body feels simultaneously relaxed and attentive, consistent yet fluid. While you deliberately intend a particular result (like activating your *will*), you're nonattached to the outcome. From this posture, your cohesion can shift into alignment with a new set of emanations. Patience, then, helps manifest your life. As your life is now concerned with developing the energy body, your impeccability generates more personal power. As a result, awareness of dreaming, *seeing,* and the other cornerstones come of its own accord.

Impeccability. You can have tremendous psychic abilities, perform dreaming and tracking beyond belief, and still not be a ranger. Being a ranger is a matter of *beingness,* a way of relating to the world, a matter of character, a matter of integrity. Yet there is no definite way to relate to the world, or to determine what character is. It is a matter of always measuring yourself through your eyes alone. In the midst of myriad different values, beliefs, realities, you're the only one who can assess your impeccability. There's a line in the British film *Cold Comfort Farm* where someone says you have "standards inside yourself." This is what I mean.

These standards are watermarks. Impeccably formed watermarks produce impeccability.

Tracking perspectives and skills were created by new-cycle Toltecs to help you develop character, which is strength of heart and mind. It is also a lack of self-reflection. As a result, it demonstrates that you're losing self-importance. To get to this point, don Juan says it calls for "frugality, thoughtfulness, simplicity, innocence." He adds that while this may sound monastic, it's not. It's just the "best use of our energy level" (*Silence,* 248).

Impeccability is forged and tempered at each stage of evolution. Impeccability for a ranger is different than for a person of knowledge. Thus you must stay open, let go of your current thoughts and feelings, and aim for greater realizations. By the time you get to be a person of knowledge, and you're no longer reflecting on the world, you've completely lost your self-importance. Then, being able to rest completely within your core means you've become a seer, which means you've totally blended your energy body with creation at large. I guess that's when impeccability arrives at the mysterious point of pure understanding.

I can write about being a person of knowledge, and I think I have a fair handle on the notion of impeccability. But I know I haven't evolved my cohesion—the actually energy of the matter—to the level of a person of knowledge. I haven't fully integrated the multidimensional experience known as "human" throughout my energy body. So part of impeccability is honest self-appraisal. This means it is also the ability to listen. The more you do, the more you naturally ease your way into other areas of your energy body—the ones you've never listened to, and thus never observed, before.

Emotional stability, calmness, and nonattachment are all signs and effects of having character, says don Juan (*Fire,* 178). These traits may also be considered as aspects of emotional intelligence. Indeed, Goleman points out that emotional intelligence may be considered as having character.[1] The foundation for intelligence, then, is knowledge of the energy body. The more you've integrated a vast number of experiences, the more you've consciously stretched through the energy body. Therefore, you get riled up less because you're affected by less. You've experienced, worked through, integrated, then moved on to the next lesson—the next batch of karmic energies. This means you're getting that much closer to your core, to that cool spot surrounded by flame. Your backbone for doing this, says don Juan, is humbleness and efficiency (*Tales,* 280).

Ethics

Ethics are governing principles of behavior: values, morals, rules. Don Juan says that ultimately what anyone does is not important. Behavior is important because we think it is, because we have learned to regard one value over another (*Separate,* 107). He, however, has cleaned his bubble of perception to approach potential impeccably, something that is beyond imagination for most of us. To get and stay there, he uses the ranger ethic. He recognizes the need for guidelines to channel energy, at least until a person is very attuned to the rhythms of Spirit and can completely let go of any discipline.

Toltecs, says don Juan, are like anybody else pursuing a vocation. They can be good or bad. In fact, since they've learned to move their focal points, they can easily injure others. But don Juan, being a modern Toltec, says we must move past ordinary considerations. Morality and beauty and must govern us. Evidently Toltecs of the old cycle were so caught up in greed and manipulation of others, they didn't even *see* invading armies coming their way. Finding an ethic based on personal freedom, rather than on the accumulation of power, was the challenge for the initial batch of new-cycle Toltecs. Part of this ethic is the practice of impeccability, which automatically gives others their freedom as well. Indeed, don Juan says a person of knowledge would never—under any circumstances—harm another person (*Silence,* 102; *Tales,* 64).

When values clash, so do people. Wars have started over very simple things: the color of skin, the shape of eyes. These days, the topic of abortion often produces a heated environment. "Right to Life" activists have even killed "Right to Choose" adherents. And there's mudslinging, arm waving, and epithet calling galore when you put someone who thinks physician-assisted suicide is ethical in the same room with someone who doesn't. Perhaps we're in the midst of our own old cycle, as we can't even *see* ourselves act completely contrary to our own beliefs.

Compassion. Compassion may be defined as "sympathy for another's misfortune." Holding to this definition, Toltecs do not have compassion. They may be able to empathize with, or to understand another's plight. They may be able to apply a lesson found in another's misfortune to their own lives, thereby avoiding the same trouble. They won't think, however, that other people are so powerless that they have to be coddled. They won't think the other person has to be changed, shown the light, or saved. People of knowledge have been born, says don Juan, from squalor. To feel sympathy in this example is like becoming accessible. Even if your feelings are for a child hustling for food, it means you don't appreciate the nature of being human. We all have personal power, and there is nothing to change in anyone (*Separate*, ch. 1).

Interesting, eh?

Okay, okay, I've got the wrong angle on compassion, you may say. If you believe compassion is honoring another's feelings, and respecting what they're experiencing without pity, then we're on the same wavelength. If it means being able to connect with another's experience without feeling responsible for it, to be able to acknowledge what *is* without judgment, then we're speaking the same language.

Even if the first consideration of compassion holds water for you, it doesn't mean Toltecs can't be kind. In fact, don Juan says that kindness is required to balance wisdom (*Fire*, 12). Remember, too, that sweetness is one of the principal moods of tracking. Understanding is actively cultivated. Toltecs are in service to others. A person of knowledge would never harm another. All of this reflects the system of behavior the new cycle came up with. It's all placed under consideration at any given crossroad. The only thing you can trust to make the best decision is your personal power. Doing so is what makes a ranger impeccable.

Power. Power gives you the ability to actively mold your world. This is why it is also one of the obstacles. You may even want to be compassionate, to change things for the better, but power will have you end up becoming a dictator. Its effects on behavior are very sneaky.

Ranger training is intended to guide you through this Herculean trial. To work through it, you need to connect with more than earthly powers. You need to fully connect with Spirit and let it guide your steps.

In essence, just remember not to *will* an outcome, even to test the possibility of being able to do so. And don't exploit others. Work with the exercises, stick with the basics, build your path. From this, any change that needs to come will come of its own accord. By not using power, you'll develop an exquisite balance. As don Juan says, there'll come a time when you have all of your resources and abilities in check, and you'll know when and how to use them. By then, you'll have become a person of knowledge (*Teachings*, 98).

Love. Just about anyone can give you a version of what love means. For some, it means you leave others alone so they may explore their own lives. For others, it means you step in to help out as often as is necessary, even if you're not asked to do so. When it comes to intimate relationships, the needle tends to go off the meter there is so much extra baggage involved. You can say you love your girlfriend, for example, but is it your sex hormones speaking up? Is it some kind of codependency that makes you feel a certain way? Do you need help paying the rent, and so you feel more open, tolerant, and loving?

Did you know that in its native Greek language, the New Testament of the Holy Bible had different words that meant different kinds of love? *Agape*, for instance, indicates a love that's more spiritual and expansive than the romantic love between people. In the first English translation, the English King James version, these different words were all reduced to one word, one spelling: love. As you might imagine, some of the clarity, flavor, and sophistication were lost.[2]

In addition, in most metaphysical environments people talk about *unconditional love*. It's difficult to get a handle on this, as everyone I've heard speak of unconditional love has placed some kind of restriction on others! You know what I mean? To actually have no restrictions, no conditions, is an amazing thing and requires intense, ongoing effort. Tapping unconditional love, as you might imagine, is part of developing a natural energy field.

Perhaps love is awareness itself, or perhaps the feeling of ongoing expansion. After all, when we fall in love, we usually become more aware, and feel as though we're stretching out. Don Juan says that seers *see* love as pink, peach, or amber. Even then, only one of these is of the human domain (*Fire*, 163–164). But heck, only three colors out of the whole batch are love? This information doesn't support a worldview in which *everything* is love.

Seems like there's a lot of confusion over this thing called love. One thing that has always made sense to me, though, was expressed by don Juan just before his student Carlos Castaneda leapt into another world, burning with the Fire from Within. Don Juan spoke eloquently of how his love for the earth had released his sadness, healed him, and eventually taught him freedom (*Tales,* 285).

PART V

TERRAINS

OF

EVOLUTION

10

"LET'S GET PHYSICAL" IS JUST AN EXPRESSION

Depending on how you look at it, the body may be viewed as a "biological organism or as a source of power," says Clara, one of Abelar's teachers.[1] Typically, we "objectively" view the body as material, as something solid. It's not all that hard to do since we use our bodies to build skyscrapers from other types of solid matter. These buildings then support us as we climb into the air. That's pretty spectacular. This type of power is also what keeps us locked in a world of material goods from which it's hard to escape to different worlds, such as a world of perception based on personal power. That is, the more personal power you have, the more you experience, the more you *see*, the more you can enter other worlds.

Traveling on an airliner, for instance, is the perception of traveling physical distance based on material kinds of power: lift, headwinds, type of engines. Teleportation, in turn, is the perception of traveling physical distance in the blink of an eye by using the energy body as the source of power. Being able to perform this ability hinges exclusively on how much personal power you have. Teleportation infuses the energy body with even more awareness, which augments *seeing*. *Seeing* then helps you connect more with your body.

By redefining the human condition as being made up of energy, you automatically give yourself more options. To participate in a world of personal power, however, you need more personal power. In this light, it's very interesting that the material world offers ways for us to enter lands of enhanced perception.

Technology

During a recent airplane trip, I sat next to a senior-level NASA engineer. We got to talking about connections between science, technology, and Toltec ways. (Yes, I was very surprised about how open and receptive he was to Toltec thought.) At times, he even talked like a Toltec. "What we don't understand," he said, "is massive compared to what we do understand."

He went on, saying that technology is learning to apply what we do know. To make it work, he said we have to make massive assumptions about reality. For example, he said that the second law of thermodynamics indicates that due to entropy there is no such thing as perpetual motion. Yet this assumption doesn't make the law true, as in Big Truth. It's just that since perpetual motion has not been experienced we can't buy into it. Hence, the social base says it does not exist. The laws of thermodynamics, then, are supports to help reduce the unknown into the known. As a result, the laws can be applied. You can then make things happen, such as making a bunch of metal fly.

As we talked about teleportation, he brought in the concept of the social base as being the prevailing reality. He said most people will have to travel on airplanes until the technology for teleportation is delivered to everyone. That is, until technology advances to the point of building

Star Trek-like transporters, the social-base reality that teaches us that we need jets to travel physical distance quickly rules our lives. It gives us our options.

Then, toward the end of our flight, he said a most compelling thing. He said that due to their ventures in space, NASA is having to think about things they've never thought about before. He added, "Once you peek into the unknown, you can't close your mind to anything."

I think that a principal difference between science and its technologies and Toltec philosophy and its technology is the way projection occurs. Scientists, for example, create highly complex theories about reality, including worldview and content; in other words, what the big picture looks like, and what pieces make up the picture. They then project that theoretical awareness outward from the personal self and onto the environment. Over time, as more and more people accept these projections, physical technologies are made manifest. While Toltecs also create highly detailed pictures, they sidestep the social aspect of manifesting. Rather than project outward, they imbue their bodies with the energy—with the intent—of their goal. Over time, the person's cohesion shifts and the potential becomes realized. The intent has been manifested. If you want to make the case that this is a process of projecting inwardly, and then manifesting that, I wouldn't argue. Inner and outward disappear at some point. Each is a matter of focus, of orientation.

As for manifesting, I think that all technologies are projections of latent capacities within the energy body. We couldn't produce a computer, for instance, unless all that knowledge was inside us. We couldn't build airplanes unless we possessed the awareness to do so. Moreover, a very gifted person can calculate mathematical formulas as fast as a computer. And don Juan can teleport his awareness. Hence we have evidence of inner and outer capacities of manifesting. Toltecs seize both options.

From personal experience, it's clear that science and technology can bolster personal evolution. Discussions like the one I had with the NASA engineer, for instance, not only add context and flavor to studying reality, but also provide different points of view regarding applications of technology. Lasers, for another example, are considered a technological advancement. They're now used for surgery, communication, and a myriad of other applications. It turns out that there are two properties of laser technology that reflect energy-body dynamics: *directionality* and *coherence*. Directionality relates to focus, as in "focused like a laser." Coherence relates to the light emanating from the device as having only one wavelength.[2] From a Toltec perspective, these properties represent focused cohesion, or unbending intent. From this comparison, you can again look at the dynamics of the energy body from different perspectives. Remember, the mark of a ranger is the ability to shift cohesion; as a result, to be able to look at the world from different points of view.

Don Juan told Castaneda that relying on mechanical devices makes us sterile. It seems Castaneda wanted to use a tape recorder for their conversations and don Juan told him he needed to beef up his body knowledge instead.[3] Given don Juan's goal of teaching Castaneda to burn with the Fire of Freedom, this makes sense. To develop that capacity requires an intense amount of training. Cultivating body knowledge helps eliminate outward projection and brings latent abilities into awareness. At the same time, however, technology might also be viewed as enhanced tracking.

For example, a crate is often used as part of the recapitulation. The idea is that by placing yourself in a box, you reduce the amount of external stimulation on the energy body. This helps you to focus and recall the specific events you're recapitulating (*Gift*, 289–290). I've found that a floatation tank—a form of technology—enhances this effect. The floatation tank was invented by John Lilly, M.D., and is featured in the film *Altered States*, which is loosely based on his explorations of consciousness.[4]

Some float tanks are shaped like coffins. A side door slides up and you ease in. Body-temperature water saturated with Epsom salts provides buoyancy. While floating, you can relax completely and not expend any energy keeping yourself afloat. When you pull the hatch closed, your environment is black and quiet. Other tanks appear more modern, such as those that are egg-shaped containers with entryways reminiscent of a hatchback automobile, or those that have large basins in soundproof rooms. With all of these, the basic premise is the same: by removing the need to offset gravity, and by depriving your awareness of physical stimulation (both of which are of the first energy field), you free up a ton of energy. You may then direct this energy into exploring the second field. The range of experiences I've had while floating includes out-of-body experiences (OBE), past-life recall, and shapeshifting.

For example, in one session I felt my awareness shift into that of a large lizard. Through sight and physical sensing, I actually experienced the world from its perspective. This experience gave me a profound respect for the awareness lizards possess. Based on my experience, I figure that they exist in a heightened awareness that comes from complete body knowledge.

In another session, I had the specific intent of having an OBE. Shortly into the session I heard a familiar tone in my left ear. Within a few moments, I heard another tone in my right ear. This one was lower in frequency. Both were steady. As the lower tone decreased, the higher-pitched tone increased and seemed like it became the entire right side of my head, not just what I was hearing. Then I entered this frequency as though I were crawling into it. As I wrapped it around my physical body, my entire body started vibrating. I found myself in my office. Then I returned to the tank. For the next half hour or so, I played with being in the tank, in my office, or simultaneously being at both places.

Virtual reality is another technology that can accelerate learning about the second field. According to the authors of *Silicon Mirage*, virtual reality is produced through a technology in which you are in two places at once: in your body, which has gadgets on it; and in your perceived reality.[5] This split away from a solely physical-world reference can serve as training wheels for exploring the second field, and how perception and learning are linked.

Indeed, there are three stages of learning in virtual reality: passive, exploratory, and interactive.[6] For the passive stage, you only absorb information. You don't have enough context or experience to do anything else. In the exploratory stage, you gain more experience, and begin to recognize what you've learned. In the interactive stage, you apply your new knowledge to create new scenarios. Virtual reality enables you to experience these stages rapidly within a highly focused and secure environment. That is, your virtual-reality sessions teach you through firsthand experience what the process of learning consists of. It seems like high-tech dreaming.

Virtual reality has a unique impact because it relies on body knowledge. Not only do you witness the virtual world you're in, but through mechanical sensors in gloves, you feel it. In fact, you guide your experience through touch. Move your finger and you redefine your world. This magic combination gives you the feeling of actually being in another world; thus, virtual reality. An excellent example of this experience may be found in the film *The Lawnmower Man*.

Expanding on this, we find that shifting the focal point produces a virtual-reality effect. For example, when you physically walk, you shift your focal point in minute increments. This shift gives you the experience of "walking."

Where your energy body is, or what part of the mind remains stationary while you have the perception of walking, I don't know, but following this line of thinking makes it easier to connect with the potential of teleportation. That is, just like walking is a shift of the focal point, teleporting the physical body is merely elevating the level of skill of physical movement. The perception of moving through time and space is just speeded up. Therefore, whether out for a walk, or popping off miles down the road in a heartbeat, the process is the same; that is, any movement is a shift in cohesion.

These technology-based applications for exploring perception affirm the value of using first-energy-field technologies. They can really give you a sense of what's afoot. However, I also recognize the wisdom in don Juan's words. Maybe our widespread use of technology is making us sterile by removing us from greater portions of our energy bodies. Maybe we should be predicting the weather based on what our energy bodies tell us, rather than based on a television show forecast. It's very startling, this kind of realization.

For the short run, perhaps the balance is to use technology, but not give your power away to it. After all, it does deliver devices that open you, allow you to explore, and thereby get the sense that something else exists. So completely leaving it behind may not be the answer. In any case, you need to foster your own personal power to make the journey. Robert Monroe, founder of TMI, would be among the first to agree.

The Monroe Institute

Since 1983, I've been associated with TMI in a variety of ways. It was then that I took their "Gateway Voyage" program in return for writing a magazine article. I guess I had a pretty good week, because I was later permitted to be a subject in their research laboratory. Over the years, I participated in another "Voyage" as well as their "Guidelines" program. The transcripts of the lab experiences and a fuller presentation of their programs are in *Traveling With Power*.

Hemi-Sync™ is a fascinating technology. It helps you travel into regions normally accessed only during sleep. For example, humans have at least four major bands of brain-wave activity: delta, theta, alpha, and beta. Although different researchers may use slightly different ranges, delta is usually .5 to 4 hertz (cycles per second), theta is 4 to 8 hertz, alpha is 8 to 13 hertz, and beta is 13-plus hertz. In very general terms, delta is a region of dreamless sleep, theta facilitates memory and intense visual imagery, alpha promotes physical relaxation and imagery, and beta is characteristic of waking consciousness. Now, all four of these brain waves are active all the time, thus producing a brain-wave cohesion. Whichever frequency is dominant, however, indicates where perception is focused. Dominant beta activity, for instance, means you're attentive to the physical world. At the same time, the map seems to change. Once, for example, OBEs were thought to occur only when delta was dominant. More recent studies suggest that an OBE can occur during other conditions.[7]

As mentioned, you may relate brain waves to cohesion. There is a "dream" cohesion, and a "wide-awake" cohesion, for example, depending on whether delta or beta is prominent. All cohesions are in the brain as well as in the energy body, and are there all the time. It's a matter of which is at the foreground—where the focal point is—that determines what is being consciously experienced. By managing cohesion, you can even enter a "dream" cohesion while totally awake. You can also create new cohesions that provide new meanings, and offer new options.

Indeed, the effect of Hemi-Sync™ on brain cohesion (and on energy-body cohesion, as one affects the other) is that your awareness is escorted into regions usually experienced only during sleep, and you are kept awake while you sojourn. In a nutshell, it works like this:

Separate tones are placed in each ear. (Research indicates that stereo headphones increase efficiency but are not required.) Let's say a 100-hertz signal is placed in the right ear, and a 104-hertz tone is then placed in the left ear. Through the brain's own mechanisms, the two tones are split and the brain resonates to the difference. This frequency is known as the *binaural beat*. The brain then entrains to, and resonates with, a 4-hertz beat. This means the dominant frequency in the brain is on the edge of delta and theta, so you're off to dreamland.

The next step is layering another set of frequencies onto the existing set. Accordingly, a 200-hertz tone and a 216-hertz tone are placed in the ears. The brain then produces a binaural beat of 16 hertz, which is in the beta range. This means you are awake and alert. The effect of having two sets of tones is that your awareness travels into the land of sleep, but you remain awake while you go there. Let the games begin!

By utilizing several layers of tones, TMI has produced a schematic of different focus levels. Focus 10, for instance, is characteristic of *mind awake, body asleep*. This is the preliminary stage for exploring. Your body feels very much asleep, yet your mind is very alert. Focus 12 is *expanded awareness*. Here, you feel lighter, more expansive, more in the mood to head off and explore. Focus 15 is *no time*, which means you can spend three hours here and it seems like only a moment or two has gone by. Focus 21 is *alternate energy systems*. This is the bridge into completely new worlds, which are often inhabited by nonhuman entities. All of TMI's seminars use these focus levels, then build on them to establish new levels.

For example, during November of 1996, I attended "Lifelines." Billed as a "soul retrieval" class, I went just for the fun of it because I really had no interest in soul retrieval. I had experienced a little of this shamanic technique years before when I helped escort several entities who had ostensibly died in Vietnam to another side of existence. As a result, I was mainly interested in checking out this new program. TMI programs had consistently quickened the pace of my growth, so deciding to go wasn't difficult. As usual, the program took on a life of its own as I settled into exploring more of my energy body with the assistance of Hemi-Sync™.

For this program, new focus levels were introduced. These levels were related to after-death experiences. Focus 22, for instance, relates to a level of existence occupied by those who have loose, random, and chaotic thoughts. People suffering from drug addiction or chronic disorientation would find themselves in this region after dying. Focus 22 pertains to those who are confused at having no body, lost souls, and the "new goners" who haven't yet figured out that they're dead.

Jumping ahead to Focus 24, is *belief system territories*. This is where like-minded people congregate. When a person dies, and he can't release his beliefs, he finds himself magnetically attracted to this level, and to an area of this level occupied by others who are dogmatically inclined in similar ways. Focus 27 is *the park*, a way station, a place of high creativity, a stepping stone to areas beyond.

I found each focus level to be a distinct environment, a stable cohesion. Because I wasn't interested in retrieving wayward souls, I spontaneously began exploring these levels in terms of beliefs and karma. As I entered each focus level, I would find myself surrounded by a rich, textured blackness. Within the blackness all sorts of things would occur. In Focus 21, I felt like I was being stretched out. I *saw* the face of an extraterrestrial, then *saw* white light as being a bridge into other worlds.

In one session, I met my father, who had died some fifteen years earlier. Rather, I perceived energy that carried the same emotional identity—the same quality of recognition—as my father. From this point, I explored whether I was really communicating with my father, whether he really did live on, whether the subliminal effects of the TMI program created a self-fulfilling prophecy, or whether I had created the experience from the fabric of pure potential. I concluded that each scenario was true in its own way. Each was an energy line that existed within infinite potential.

During this session, one participant reported that she saw an extraterrestrial who said, "It's time to act like a global society." Another participant had a life review of "shitty stuff," convincing him he had to work on his life and get his act together. Yet another person experienced a "Field of Last Memories," defined as a stage of dying, but not necessarily complete death.

In another session, I said to no one in particular, but to all creation, "Show me my fate." I *saw* an energy body, then *saw* emanations and their connections with each other. The emanations were like strands of light energy, with each strand a separate part of creation. Between the strands was diffuse light, like the way light fills a room. Yet, since everything was light, it all seemed to be made of the same substance. Indeed, the entire universe contained intelligence, awareness that was represented as light. I then had the thought that all these focus-level shifts were lateral shifts of the focal point. They were necessary to know the entire energy body, and to offer a sense of relation to the third energy field.

In one session, I rode on the back of a whale. We dove deep within the ocean. Then it went into a golden tunnel, and entered a dimension of pure thought-energy. Here, thoughts and feelings merged to produce perceptions that reflected each other. I became a creator. In another session, I noticed people milling about. They were all wearing the same style of clothing: drab grey for their drab minds. This particular session occurred in Focus 22. I deliberately left this area, as it felt counter-productive. Actually, it's easy to shift levels. Once you get a handle on how to shift, you can go from 12 to 27, or 22 to 15, whatever your intent. To arbitrarily say something must occur at a specific level automatically creates a dull mind, a Focus-22 mentality.

At the same time, at least until people grew accustomed to a level, their experiences related what the focus level was initially described as. My experiences in Focus 27, for example, were more abstract than when I was in Focus 22. Whereas I would perceive disoriented people in Focus 22, in Focus 27 I would perceive bundles of energy. Each bundle carried some kind of intelligence. By relating one to another, I gained intuitive realizations. During one session my awareness bounced like a billiard ball among these bundles. By the time I slowed down my movement, centered myself, and gained better control, I had the sense that if a person can't release enough beliefs, her energy stays in a specific zone. When this energy gathers even more energy, it expresses itself as another life—a life reflecting the level it came from. Hence, the energy would reincarnate. However, if she could release these constellations of energy, she would break the wheel of rebirth. She would forever escape the gravity that pulls awareness back into life as we commonly know it.

Most of the participants joyfully tried their hand at soul retrieval. Some reported retrieving parts of themselves, becoming a bit more whole. Others felt that they had actually communicated with a deceased entity, and then helped the entity to a better place.

Keep in mind that the different experiences of soul retrieval could be the result of the projection of karmic beliefs or patterns. This is how projection works. It shapes how we experience something; nay, *everything*. Variations in karma could account for the variations in the experiences these people reported. Whatever the case, it all makes me wonder. You can't beat that.

Time

If you're engaged in soul retrieval, you're more than likely to assume that the deceased entity, his earthly life, and your experience with him, flow in a straight line. If you're in 2010 and the entity died in 1948, you can better relate to his disorientation because you have knowledge of that period in history—be it from personal experience or from books. I know this is a very broad-stroke picture, but it's useful. A linear, sequential structure of time works well to help increase the chances of a successful mission. Relating soul retrieval to a familiar reference makes it easier to find a dead person who is disoriented and usher him to the promised land.

When dealing with reincarnation, you assume a person lives, dies, and gets reincarnated along a certain continuum. It's in the nature of language and the word "reincarnation" that guides perception to the avenue known as "the straight line of time." So a person is born in 1702, dies in 1754, and reincarnates in 1910. That's a typical scenario. It makes sense if we're going to "re" our awareness. Plus, to begin getting a handle on reincarnation, it's often best to relate it to the known world. In this case, a linear pattern of time is part of the known world. It's what most people grow up with. It's how we learn to "tell time." The more you open up, however, the more things change. One of these is time.

For instance, the more people get a handle on reincarnation, the more they open up to the idea of multiple, simultaneous incarnations. Indeed, most people experience this pattern as they unfold their consciousness. Watch people and pay attention to how their view of time and space changes as they get more involved with meditation, for instance. Maybe you've even watched yourself change.

Anyway, simultaneous incarnations means that you have a bunch of lives that are all occurring at the same moment. Whether you perceive a past, a future, or a current life depends on where you're focused. You might say that each separate life is a cohesion of "All Time."

In short, then, simultaneous time, linear time, and all variations of time exist. They are all illusions as well. How you experience time results from your focus, from your brain-wave pattern, from your energy body cohesion, from the location of your focal point.

When you stop the world, you bring to bear a very unusual focus of time. In the *Star Trek: The Next Generation* episode "Journey's End," for example, young Wesley Crusher stops the world with the help of the Traveler (a very Toltec kind of guy). In so doing, a battle among the Cardasians, Federation troops, and native villagers stops in mid-motion. The Traveler and Crusher freeze-frame the world, and pull themselves out of the social base of time, the time everyone else is focused in. Then they just step out of the picture, literally, enter a new experience, and let everyone else go about their business of fighting. It's all in the wrist of focus.

The Null Point

The *null point* is a corridor of power. It's a zero point of perception. It's a gateway into enhanced awareness. It's an opening to your core. It's the essence of nonpatterning.

It's also part of the perceptual map being created by TMI. Body polarity actually switches when a person hits this sweet spot. This means that it's between focus levels; hence, between form. Then again, it may be a specific Focus level itself.

From a Toltec perspective, the null point may also be related to the focal point of "no pity." For instance, when you're there you won't feel like helping others. Rather, you won't feel as though you *have* to help.

Being of service is a tracking technique to help you open up perception. It's an ethic—a value—to help start energy flowing in non-self-important ways. The more you reduce self-importance, the more you grow. Therefore losing self-importance is very selfish. But when you're at the point of no pity, being of service or not really doesn't matter all that much. You just continue to be of service as a matter of training. You still behave that way; you're just not attached to the behavior—or its results. On the flip side, when you stray from the point of no pity, reorienting yourself to being of service helps restore that focal point position. That's what the exercise and training are for, to get you to a point where a whole new dynamic takes place.

Now then, the null point is just such a place. Imagine you're in a corridor. On each side of the hallway are doors. Let the corridor represent the null point, and each door represent some kind of realization. For instance, say you want to study physics. To get the best advantage, you need to place yourself at the null point of "physics." If you don't, you're just rehashing what you already know. You can get to the focal point of "I remember this or that, therefore it has to be true" anytime you want. But to learn, to really stretch out and learn, then get thy butt to the null point. You need to shed what you think you know to learn something new. To do this takes a heaping helping of nonpatterning. You also need to know what you're looking for—at least it helps. It keeps energy focused to speed up the learning, and the arriving at what you're trying to learn. In short, it speeds up the knowing.

Typically, your "heaping helping of nonpatterning" seemingly gets you nowhere. Don't worry, you're just fooling around in the unknown, so how can you know anything? With patience, one fine day you'll tap the null point, and will have enough experience with nonpatterning to recognize it. There just happens to be an infinite number of doors in the null point corridor, however. One for astronomy, another for relationships, yet another for sex, for biology, for hairballs, for lions and tigers and bears, for music. . . . Find the door you want. In this case, it's "Science." The next step is to intend your awareness through the door. Once inside, you're in the general energy of science, which offers an overview of the entire field, or you can be in another corridor! Perhaps it's the nonpatterning corridor of physics. Once in this aisle, you're centered in the energy you want to explore. This time, the doors are labeled "Quantum," "Mechanical," "Newtonian," "Relativity," "Particles," . . . Pick a topic and enter that door to learn more about that discipline.

Again, inside these doors you can explore the topic, or bring yourself back to a null-point corridor to get even more specific. Scholars love this stuff. You don't even have to go backward and open and close doors, walk down hallways, and follow a trail of breadcrumbs back to where you started. You just shift your awareness. Shift your energy. Shift your cohesion. You end up where you place your attention. Therefore, your intention starts and ends the journey.

In some environments, a small push of intent can produce large results. For instance, in chaos theory there's something called *sensitive dependence of initial conditions*. It means that very small differences in input can become extremely large differences in output. That is, minute changes can have dramatic results. One example is that a very minor change in weather in one part of the globe can significantly alter weather patterns all over the planet. From heart disease to weather, it maps out irregular patterns—or at least what seems to be irregular. In this light, "irregular" means that scientists don't yet have a wide enough picture to predict what is under scrutiny; thus, it's chaotic in relation to the current known world.[8] Chaos theory is spinning the world anew as it accounts for things that classical science doesn't.

Taking the liberty of applying this theory to consciousness, we find that the point from where you begin has a huge impact on what you experience, even to the degree of forming entire realities. If you believe the world is concrete, then you increase the odds of going through a door to that world. Just this one belief does not an entire world create. But since you have hooked into an intent associated with that larger reality, it might have the effect of hooking you to the larger intent. Therefore, you have begun from a very small starting point but have ended up in a very large world.

Taking further liberty, let's define chaos theory as a tool to map second-energy-field patterns. After all, many dream states such as teleportation are irregular, at least to proponents of nondreaming realities. Now then, say that one effect of mapping the second field is that you devise a technology that can isolate, define, and predict dreaming energies. Doing so helps you prove your theory. Okay, fine. But as soon as you acknowledge this, and everyone comes around to agreeing with it, your theory becomes part of first-energy-field order. It becomes part of the social-base known world. You've now enhanced your worldview and, as a result, the perspective that chaos theory predicts second-field energies becomes obsolete. After all, you've now placed it in the first field. Perhaps a better scenario might be that part of your new known world is that you have a device that can accurately map unknown regions of the energy body, including those of the first and second fields, and that it can do so by relating what is found to the known world. After all, both energy fields are infinite.

Whew! Let's take a break. Perhaps all this mental machination is why don Juan says that Toltecs make meticulous maps of their world, then laugh at them and move on.

Behind each door, then, is a bubble of perception, a room full of mirrors. Returning time and time again to the null point—to pure nonpatterning—helps you burst the bubble and reveal a new vision—yes, a new bubble.

Therefore, to continue to learn, you need to be able to return to potential. Otherwise, you stay within the corridors of what you already know. Indeed, without the null point, and hence without the ability to stop the world, all consciousness-enhancing systems are just half-baked schemes for mapping an active dream life. If you can't break free from the manifest world and tap potential, you'll remain locked within the beauty of your own doings—and will absolutely love being in jail. The null point is the threshold for stopping the world, which means you can reach potential. You can literally step out of the realizations you currently occupy. This is why it's important to play with potential. It helps kick off the voyage into the void, which might turn out to be a voyage into, through, and beyond potential.

☡ ☡ ☡

Physical technologies, to reiterate, are first-energy-field productions. They may have their roots in imagination and the second field, but putting them out there in the world makes them part of the first field. As such, they are projections of energy that have such force behind them that they've become material. As elements of first-field tracking, they're also tools originating from total awareness to help us claim freedom.

Part of this journey is learning that your physical body—indeed, the entire world you're now experiencing—is just one very large cohesion, one band of energy. It is "physical" because we have agreed that it is so. But it's only as physical—only as concrete—as you want it to be. There are more worlds, more options, than you can imagine. The physical world is just an expression, just another dream.

11

IN
YOUR
DREAMS

Dreaming, from a Toltec perspective, is a way to explore the second energy field. By doing so, you discover dreams beyond the dream of the everyday world. Indeed, when handled with utmost skill, dreaming is a journey to your core.

Arriving fully at your core requires discharging an immense amount of karma. One way to do this is to command numerous cohesions. For this, you must be able to stabilize cohesions as well as break the fixations that hold them in place. Dreaming, approached and applied in a step-by-step manner, delivers this workout.

The tracking of the matter is to bring knowledge back from dreamland and express it in the physical world, a traditional shamanic maneuver. For instance, Castaneda uses dreaming to write his books,[1] and don Genaro uses teleportation to move through physical time and space as though he were in a dream (*Tales,* 48).

Hooking dreaming into a variety of practical applications stretches and stabilizes you throughout your energy body, and so speeds up your evolution. What "practical" means to you is something for you to figure out. To me, writing is very practical. But how about building a machine that teleports people? That's a pretty wild idea, and may not seem very practical by today's standards. But if you could learn how to teleport your awareness, couldn't that knowledge be expressed in the physical world using some type of technology?

In dreaming, you work directly with cohesion. There are no procedures, no step-by-step manuals to apply pressure to the energy body. You used those to build a foundation, and set the stage for dreaming. Now, the pressure to shift into dreaming and explore it comes from your intent. The dramatic shifts in cohesion that dreaming supplies give you more to witness, experience, *see*, and consider. Once again, this speeds your evolution when handled properly. Otherwise, you may lose yourself in your adventures.

Accelerating your evolution is what tracking freedom is all about. However, just plugging yourself in to the fast track may prove damaging. You might succumb to power, or maybe you'll get lost in the second field just like the old-cycle Toltecs. Preventing these maladies is where tracking skills save the day. Through nonpatterning, for instance, you can suspend movement and, as a result, remove yourself from your fast-track momentum. You may then give yourself a breather to make sure you're oriented properly, or, by using the model of stages to measure your steps, you generate more strength of mind and peace of heart.

Because dreaming places you in heightened awareness, you can also learn from your journeys more readily. By stepping outside the first field, you're not subject to its pushes and pulls. As a result, perception is more fluid, flexible, and free. For example, you may enter dreaming to learn advanced *seeing* practices, such as *seeing* the Eagle's emanations. Toltecs of the old days did this to not experience spontaneous combustion. Seems like tapping the amount of energy in an emanation through the physical body alone can literally blow it up (*Fire*, 183).

Therefore, just like computer software speeds up calculations, dreaming can bestow huge amounts of experience, then help you compare and contrast those experiences to generate knowledge. Over time, dreaming can also help you generate wisdom. All of this combined is what helps you beat the rap of falling off the tuna boat.

By tracking dreaming, over the centuries Toltecs have produced a map of dreaming cohesions. These cohesions may also be considered levels of, or degrees of competency with, dreaming. The following is a brief outline of them, with a few modifications based on personal experience.

Dreaming Cohesions

Entering a level of dreaming is changing the energy body to the vibration of that cohesion, bringing it into phase, so to speak. You then produce the perception of that order, and of the experiences available from within that cohesion. In addition, each level represents a greater degree of heightened awareness. Therefore, success hinges on how much personal power you have.

Finding success means that you've integrated within your energy body the various energies—all the watermarks—of a complete cohesion. Each cohesion has the karma of its lessons contained within it. Integrate those and you're ready for the next level. The practices for this consolidation are entering a cohesion, then traveling within it. Indeed, notice that odd-numbered levels deal with entering a new domain; even-numbered levels deal with stabilizing, or learning to handle, that domain.

In *The Art of Dreaming*, don Juan mentions seven dreaming levels, or *gates*. However, Castaneda ends his dissertation at the fourth stage. Putting pieces of the puzzle together, in *A Toltec Path* I conjecture about what I think the remaining three consist of. Over time, I have found that this schematic holds water, even if it's not exactly what don Juan had in mind. In addition to these, I offer personal considerations about two more levels. They're based on continued exploration of don Juan's map for burning with the Fire of Freedom, as well as recapitulating the effects don Juan had on my energy body.

Level One: Entering Dreaming. What separates ordinary dreams from dreaming is that in dreaming you're awake. Dreams are like watching a movie. Dreaming is actually stepping into the movie, being a part of it. Just because you enter a "sleep" cohesion doesn't mean you can't be awake. We've just learned that we're supposed to shut down awareness when we go to sleep, but sleep is a natural way to shift into dreaming, and a way to strengthen cohesion-shifting muscles. Your dreams will remain in the land of ordinariness, however, if you don't apply intent. That is, unless you intend to enter dreaming, you're not bringing your personal power into focus. As a result, you'll experience difficulty breaking the barrier of becoming awake within your dreams; *lucid dreaming*, it's often called.

As you slide off to sleep and your cohesion begins to shift, anything you have been holding on to may enter your awareness. Since this includes your fears and concerns, you might want to turn off the show. On the very threshold of dreaming, it is quite common for people to turn away, and intend sleep. Therefore, overcome this by facing up to whatever you're experiencing.

There is a point, a very narrow margin of perception, where you can either enter dreaming or fall off into the blackness of sleep. For no particular reason, I call it the *dew point*. The dew point is the null point of dreaming. It's a hinge made up of nothing, but which allows you to apply intent. It's not necessary to find the dew point to enter dreaming. You can sidestep it and still shift your cohesion. I just want to point out a few things you might encounter as you try your hand at this game. If you do find it, you can use it to spin your awareness into dreaming proper. Allow your intent to bring images out of the blackness, then establish a bridge into the images. After this, let yourself flow into the images, and into the dream.

Having a purpose for dreaming helps lubricate this transition. For instance, a few times I've mentioned using dreaming to write. This may be a suitable purpose for you as well. Or, perhaps you'd just like to explore randomly. Whatever resonates strongly within you, use it to mount dreaming energies. Don't be bashful. Figure out what you want, what is part of your path with heart, then go for it.

Quite often, you'll experience a surge of energy when you're on the brink of dreaming. This is your cohesion shifting, and this shift in energy may translate itself through the physical body as intense, raw emotion. This may make you very uncomfortable, or may simply surprise you. Either way, you'll probably work hard to restabilize your normal cohesion and end the experience. For most people, letting go is the difficult part of stage one.

Level Two: Dreaming Travel. Okay, now you're inside a dream. What the heck do you do now? Learn to travel, advises don Juan. A way to do this is to find scouts from another world, the inorganic world. For this, he gives an exercise of deliberately changing your dream. That is, you isolate a feature of your dream, then use it to form a new dream, like television shows spin off a character from one show to make a new show (*Dreaming*, 44). You may then isolate, or discover, inorganic scouts as a feature in your dreams.

Don Juan maintains that the inorganic world is inhabited by intelligent, sentient beings. They're just not carbon-based intelligence as are humans and other organic life forms of this world. Finding scouts from this world serves several purposes. For one, you let them escort you into new dimensions. In the same manner that your parents helped teach you to walk, this is how you may learn to travel in dreaming. Plus, this is a huge test for weaknesses. If you pass, he says you head to the next level (*Dreaming*, 108, 111). If you don't pass, perhaps you'll become a petty tyrant, full of yourself and your grand accomplishments, and never really learn how to handle your energy body. Sounds a lot like dealing with the obstacles of clarity and power, doesn't it?

The ability to control dreaming also gives you hands-on demonstrations of manifesting. Since dreams are not subject to the influences of normal time and space that affect physical landscapes, you can significantly speed up, or slow down, any scenario. Paying attention to what unfolds offers lessons that you can bring back and apply within your daily, physical world. The general idea of level two, however, is to gain further command over cohesions. By shifting dreams, and by traveling within them, you increase your skill in energy management.

Level Three: The Dreaming Body. At this stage, the energy body is ready to act, says don Juan. Dreaming begins to merge with the physical world (*Dreaming*, 142).

The effect on perception is that you produce the dreaming body, or have what many call an out-of-body experience. I really don't think anything leaves the physical body, although there is the perception of "going out" as the term suggests. Rather, as cohesion shifts, the movement of energy is translated by consciousness as movement of a second, nonphysical body. This second body then feels like it leaves the physical body. But the perception of second-body movement just echoes the movement of the focal point to another position.

A distinct advantage of having dreaming-body experiences is that they help break the fixations of the physical world. The energy body becomes more supple, and more manageable. All in all, because you're working with the entire energy body, you get a better picture of what it means to be human.

Level Four: Dreaming-Body Travel. Just as you learned to travel within a dream in level two, now you get to travel using the dreaming body. During level three, your dreaming body typically ends up anywhere and everywhere, depending on how your cohesion shifts. At level four, you learn locomotion skills. You learn to pinpoint your OBE travels. As a result, you can explore other dimensions, or take trips to your favorite places in this world.

Level Five: The Double. All of your dreaming generates personal power. So by the time you reach this level, your energy body is such a powerhouse that some people notice your second body and think it's your physical body. This is what don Juan meant when he told Castaneda that sometimes the person he talked with was not don Genaro but rather his double (*Tales,* 48).

Level Six: Teleportation. Remember that don Juan said level three is when dreaming and physical realities begin to merge? Well, at this stage of the ball game, you can further connect your first and second energy fields and then intend the whole package to precise locations in your physical world. Relating your travels to the physical world not only binds your first and second fields, but it gives you a consistent reference—a home port—from which to travel further. One ability stemming from these travels is teleportation, just like don Genaro when he beams himself to a mountaintop in the blink of an eye. Teleportation, then, is a matter of mind, not of distance.

Don Juan makes the case that don Genaro can do this type of thing when he is dreaming. As a result, he says don Genaro can do "more than if he were awake" (*Fire,* 237). The double is not bound by physical constraints. However, if the physical body is also energy, then isn't it possible to apply everything found through dreaming to it? Isn't it possible to teleport the physical body just as don Genaro teleports his double?

Evidence exists that this is so. For instance, Castaneda reports that he and the Little Sisters (female apprentices to don Juan) entered dreaming and disappeared from the physical world. Evidently, they had difficulty returning. They were brought back to full awareness by the Genaros (male apprentices to don Juan) dumping buckets of water on them. This helped reconstitute their ghostlike images back into physical matter (*Second Ring,* ch. 6).

Now, we can talk about dreaming until the cows come home, but it won't get us anywhere. It is by dreaming that we gain actual experiences with cohesion. This, in turn, enables the body to store and to bring about these abilities.

Levitation, for example, is an aspect of level six, as it suspends the physical law of gravity. Rather than beam off to a mountaintop, you float in the air, and not just with your dreaming body, either. Several years ago, I levitated. After the initial stages of this spontaneous occurrence, I was able to *will* my physical legs up and down several times. Each time my legs rose, I floated freely. I have to tell you, this kind of experience changes your point of view.

The concept of burning with the Fire of Freedom describes the physical body transcending—resurrecting, as it were—this physical world. Looking at this from a Toltec point of view, don Juan wouldn't have been able to burn with the Fire had he not gained such control over his energy body that his entire physical body became only one of many manageable cohesions. Accordingly, level six is exercise for entering the third energy field.

Level Seven: The Fire from Within. You have heard people say we only use a small percentage of our brain? Well, in like manner, we only use a small percentage of our energy bodies. To go completely past the Eagle, you must first become one with it. To merge with energy that intense must be why the old-timers used to experience the "spontaneous combustion" cohesion. Keep in mind that this might be a risk for you as well since by tracking freedom you're activating your entire energy body. You must do this to become one with the Eagle.

What happens along the way is anyone's guess. Don Juan says that it's possible to stabilize focal point positions that are not of this world. Doing so, however, increases the risk of getting trapped in those worlds. He says that to avoid this pitfall, new-cycle Toltecs learned not to stabilize any focal point position permanently except that of heightened awareness. Experiencing other worlds became only a technique to learn about cohesion. This knowledge enables an alignment with the Eagle that brings all the energy within you to life. This act of *will* produces freedom (*Fire,* 294–295).

Level Eight: Freedom Travel. The idea here is that once you're in the third field, maybe there's an exercise to handle it better. And maybe that exercise is learning to return to Earth. You would then have a reference point to explore the immensity of the third field. You could launch, explore, return, assimilate your findings, and take off again. This would make the third field concrete, usable.

I think don Juan does this. I also think that the ability to master the bridge between the human domain and the third field is what separates Toltecs—even the very best of the new cycle—from seers.

Level Nine: Beyond the Light. Just as a Toltec gets his fill of this world, and gleefully bounds into the third field, perhaps the seer gets his fill of the third field, and wants to move on. Therefore, just to keep the door open, I submit that there is a ninth level, a level that builds on the sense of freedom, and delivers awareness to . . .

Dreaming and the Chakras

Think of chakras as dimensions of awareness, as arenas of consciousness that contain their own landscapes. Also, think of them as energies that may correspond to dreaming levels.

Chakra One. Raw energy. Primal awareness. Becoming aware of this power pack is like becoming aware that other dimensions exists, such as keeping yourself awake while entering dreaming.

Chakra Two. When you perceive two dimensions, you have the beginning of a relationship. You can sense things about you. Dreaming level two deals with travel, and you can't travel without relation. If you didn't have another point of awareness, how could you travel, or be aware of movement?

This emotional center is often related to the adrenal glands. When you get charged up, or endangered, adrenaline kicks in to save the day. Given the emotional surges that occur during the onset of dreaming, perhaps the two are connected in this way as well.

Chakra Three. Your physical body is perceived as three-dimensional, and with it you perceive the world as 3-D. Dreaming level three develops the dreaming body, which is typically perceived as a 3-D body. That is, due to our daily habits, the dreaming body often resembles the physical body. It might also assume the shape of an animal, or a sphere of energy, all of which are 3-D.

In essence, however, the dreaming body is a point of awareness. It emanates from the first chakra, from initial awareness. The sense of separate dimensions results from the interplay of different energies. That is, while all energies are essentially of one source energy, different states of energy produce relationships within ourselves as well as with the source.

As an aside, have you ever considered that our solar system has a yellow sun, just like the third chakra is yellow? And that Earth is the third planet from the sun? And that, just like the effect of chakra three, we can't seem to get out of our thoughts long enough to be aware of anything but ourselves?

No? Well, have you ever thought that we're now opening up to worlds beyond ours (such as extraterrestrial worlds) as the ozone layer is being depleted? Do you think that the reduction of this protective energy is allowing energies from outside of our little home to enter our world and saturate our awareness? Is this making us awaken to them? Anyway . . .

Chakra Four. The heart chakra is where you begin to step outside of your 3-D self; you gain the perception of being connected with your environment. Remember, you always were connected; now you perceive it.

In terms of dreaming, at level four you begin to express dreaming in your physical world, in the environment of your physical body. Your expertise in dreaming-body travel begins to hook together your dreaming world and your physical world.

Chakra Five. The fifth chakra embodies communication, a form of merging with another consciousness. Resulting from your 3-D energies, you can talk about yourself. Add the fourth dimension and you can talk with others about your environment. This means you are gaining perspective and control of your environment. It also means you can talk incessantly about new forms of yourself, making it another entrance into the woolly world of self-importance.

At this stage, the dreaming-body acts. It is the time of the double. This means your dreaming body is developing movement. Therefore, you are gaining more perspective and control. As a result, you can move about in the physical world, and communicate with others, by using the double. Perhaps this is why this energy is called the "double," as you get double the fun, double the trouble.

Chakra Six. This is the capstone of the second set of three-dimensional energies. Chakras one through three form the physical body, as least that's how it's perceived. Chakras four through six form the complete double. Teleportation, then, means you have refined your skills of moving the double in the physical world. Two sets of energies hooked together to enable a most remarkable "double" relationship with the world.

Chakra Seven. This chakra is on the crown of the head, the last chakra within the normal human area, which means it resides on and within the physical body.

Burning with the Fire from Within means you have gained control of these energies, and you're stepping out into other worlds. However, to illustrate a very important point, let's again separate the Fire from Within from the Fire of Freedom. You may burn with the Fire from Within and remain within the human condition as Toltecs define it; that is, remain within the energy body. You may shift your cohesion so greatly that you evaporate from this world, but remain within the second field. This is what happened to the old cycle. Burning with the Fire of Freedom is a very special version of the Fire from Within. It is shifting completely and unerringly into the third energy field, to a domain of energy outside the human energy body.

Chakra Eight. Located just above the head, this chakra is removed from the ordinary human world, but remains within the energy body. Control of this energy means you can step in and out of the ordinary world. By shifting cohesion completely to it, you'd burn with the Fire from Within. You could then return by another significant shift. Again, however, just because you can do this doesn't mean you've learned the Fire of Freedom.

Chakra Nine. The white light. God, for some. The human mold, for others. The source of all country-western songs (not to mention R&B), which means it contains all vibrations in the human world, be they musical or otherwise. This chakra is the bridge between the human world—ordinary and nonordinary—and whatever lies beyond. For Toltecs, whatever lies beyond is the third field. Therefore, getting a handle on this energy is your steppingstone to freedom.

The Inorganic World

Referring back to dreaming level two, don Juan says that the inorganic world is a testing ground where you learn how to handle power, the toughest obstacle of all the stages. Castaneda, for example, was tempted by inorganic beings to learn telekinesis. All he had to do was sign over his soul, so to speak. Fortunately, he resisted (*Dreaming,* 115).

On occasion, during dreaming, I have entered their world. Consistent with don Juan's teachings, I found that these creatures live in a labyrinth of tunnels. Once, I was at a spot where I could head in the direction of any one of several tunnels. I picked the larger, and just as I entered I met a group of beings. Their appearance was not solid. Their bodies shifted about. At times they looked ghastly and ghostly, other times thin-framed, almost humanoid. At yet other times, they seemed waiflike, like an image that can never be brought into focus. As soon as I noticed them, they came toward me and hovered about my body, asking me what I wanted. I felt simultaneously interested, entertained, and repelled. I felt don Juan's energy, and remembered his admonition to be very careful in this land. So I left the tunnel, which ended my dreaming.

Getting back to the idea of the inorganic world as testing ground, in it you can learn to shape your dreamscapes at *will*. This is not unlike learning to do so in lucid dreaming. Actually, a case could be made that visits to the inorganic world occur in lucid dreams. Anyway, by fooling around with this ability, you either get to a point where it is no fun determining the outcome of your adventures, or you get lost in controlling your world.

In terms of power as an obstacle, if you can't let go, you're experiencing the illusion of control. In fact, you're not controlling anything. You're falling off the tuna boat, and not awakening anything deeper within your energy body than this level. Therefore, one attitude to help you handle power is to consider daily life as a lucid dream. To grow beyond this level, you need to let life reign, not your self-importance. Even if life itself is a huge projection, to track freedom you must grow beyond the limits of each level of projection.

Elemental Spirits

Although they are inorganic, many elemental spirits I have met are not of the inorganic world don Juan speaks of. They don't contrive to cement your allegiance. They don't entice you with plays of power.

They do communicate, teaching me a little about their worlds, and more about the world humans occupy. Years ago, for example, I met an elemental who calls herself Xena (zee-nah). She is small enough to sit on my shoulder, looks solid and transparent at the same time, and looks and feels feminine. Indeed, except for those wings on her back, she looks like a tiny, luminous human. So perhaps she is a fairy.

From time to time, she tells me of her world. Sometimes I *see* part of her world, a maze of tunnels. I *see* these tunnels superimposed over river or creek embankments. I used to think I could contact her only at places of running water. More recently, however, I felt her presence while walking in my wooded backyard. Looking about the yard, or rather feeling about the yard, I *saw* her fly up to me. Poised motionless in midair, we had a short talk. She then introduced me to The Keeper.

Elementals are typically associated with physical aspects of nature: plants, minerals, and water, for example. Their existence speaks to the intelligence the entire world contains. Just as your body contains different forms of intelligence, the world at large offers a variety pack of different intelligences. Learning how to dream teaches you how to bring that awareness into your daily life.

Extraterrestrials

Once you learn dreaming travel, there are yet other types of intelligent life you may visit, such as extraterrestrials (ETs). Don Juan says the overriding impact of the inorganic world is that it demolishes your reason. Maybe contact with other kinds of intelligent life that are out of this world performs the same effect. If this is true, perhaps we can bypass the seductions of the inorganic world and visit ETs to accomplish the same result.

It might also be a good way to learn Toltec-like lessons. For instance, several ETs once pulled me into an OBE. Now, your body needs the experience of something to turn mental concepts into knowledge. That is, you can talk about OBEs all day long, but until you thoroughly experience them, and integrate them, your knowledge remains just a bunch of talk. Through body knowledge, you learn how to shift cohesion. Talking may give you the notion of how it's done, even point you in the right direction, but it doesn't—by itself—let you purposefully shift cohesion.

In addition, ET culture offers lessons in perception. Take UFOs, for example. Regular time machines, they are. Evidently, some ETs have produced a technology that accounts for, and produces, dreaming practices. They've taken innate capacities of the energy body, and projected them into the first field, just like we've done with computers. Dreaming level six, or teleportation, if you recall, is where you turn your body into a time machine. You pull yourself out of the normal flow of time, and pop off to distances that it would take hours to walk or drive to. You pull yourself out of the first field, enter the second field, travel, then return to the first—all in the blink of an eye. This is mere practice for doing the same thing in relation to the third field, and dreaming level eight.

As humans evolve, perhaps the eighth chakra will become the crown chakra. As a result, we will have become an entirely new species. We'll look different, act different, think different, the whole nine yards. Maybe our eyes will be larger, like the eyes of the ETs we see in movies. If so, maybe we'll see new colors, like Enon, the color of the eighth chakra. Surely we'll see this color on the outer edge of rainbows. Move over, Dorothy!

All this is in the works, or should I say in the workings? Indeed, it is all part of the ever-present scheme of the universe. Stepping outside normal time, we find that it's all happening right now, even if we aren't aware of it. Enon, for example, is already part of rainbows. Our eyes just haven't evolved to the point of being able to handle that frequency, at least on a physical level. So perhaps dreaming also gives us a glimpse of our future selves, our ETness.

Near-Death Experiences

As mentioned in chapter seven, I first began hanging out with ETs in TMI's laboratory. Every time we used a 4-hertz binaural beat, I would contact an ET intelligence that identified itself as being from the Pleiades. One day I asked the monitors of the lab session for a different binaural beat. So we used 1.5 hertz. As soon as I centered myself, I found myself in a tunnel heading toward white light. I was having a clinically induced *near-death experience* (NDE).

Experiences with white light, and meetings with inhabitants of that energy, are often part and parcel of an NDE. This is where don Juan takes exception to the normal interpretation, however. People typically say they've met God, talked with Jesus, experienced unconditional love, and felt totally complete. Don Juan says these people feel complete because they've met the human mold, the embodiment of "all that is human." Indeed, by doing so, how could you not feel complete? By repeated exposure to this energy, don Juan says you dissipate the passion of it, and discover a new interpretation. That is, it is not God, but the human mold—only one very small emanation in all creation. God is of a greater glory.

I had my first NDE when I was about eight years of age. I almost drowned. While it made no sense to me at the time, after being rescued I began *seeing* visions. The fact is that NDEs are often reported as being real eyeopeners, often third-eye openers.

It is also interesting to note that tunnels are frequently reported as part of an NDE. As mentioned, tunnels are also part of the inorganic world, and at least one elemental-spirit world. Perhaps tunnels, then, are avenues of perception, rather than concrete formations. Maybe they are a perceptual effect of being able to channel awareness along specific paths. The ability to form and channel energy then produces the perception of tunnels.

In dreaming states such as an NDE, a person enters heightened awareness. As a result, you don't have to struggle to produce rarified perceptions. In this instance, rarified perception pertains to witnessing out-of-this-world events, such as inorganic life, ETs, NDEs, OBEs, or whatever; all of which are in the fabric of dreaming.

ꝑ ꝑ ꝑ

The true goal of dreaming, says don Juan, is to perfect the energy body (*Dreaming,* 42). Remember, the goal is not to simply enter mind-boggling worlds. The primary goal is to use these experiences to evolve your energy into a natural field, and remain in heightened awareness. The training is to become a seer, not a wizard. It just so happens that a wizardly lifestyle is part of a Toltec path, but the path is also that of the seer.

A perfected energy body, then, contains energy that is perfectly matched with the Eagle's emanations. One effect is that you are simultaneously totally here, totally an individual, and totally not here, totally part of all that is around you. This is what I *saw* in don Juan. His energy body delicately and exquisitely matched the fibers of light that were outside of him. This is also a way of saying that he had developed a natural energy field. He had learned to *be*, completely.

PART VI

THE
ESSENCE
OF
EVOLUTION

12

LIVING IN INFINITE POTENTIAL

Potential is the crack between worlds. It is the full force of all creation. It contains everything, while being nothing other than itself. Yet it is infinite. It is a state of energy from which all realizations arise—be they intellectual or material.

The core of your energy body is part and parcel of this magical, mysterious force. Your core connects directly, intimately, with potential, and all your cohesions are realizations generated by it. The trick is to burn off the karma within the energy body, and fully bring your core to the foreground of awareness. Doing so awakens you completely. I refer to this intensity of experience as *being*.

Being

Being consists of maintaining a natural vibration, an ebb and flow between self and world, a grand harmony of energies within and without. In this exquisite state, you have a greater sense of self, a lightness of emotion, and a calm clarity that fills you with meaning. There is also a sense of oneness with all creation, and a feeling of having a personal place in the world. Yet this rhythm automatically carries with it the experience of nonattachment. As a result, the cosmos becomes, paradoxically, impersonal: the ultimate position of "no pity."

One characteristic of *being* is experiencing *flow*. The notion of *flow* is explored in the groundbreaking book by Mihaly Csikszentmihalyi, titled *Flow: The Psychology of Optimal Experience*. Csikszentmihalyi says that joy, creativity, and total involvement with life are all aspects of *flow*, and are all conditions of optimal experience.[1] Furthermore, Goleman says that entering *flow* is "emotional intelligence at its best."[2]

Accordingly, entering *flow* and *being* is not a haphazard, far-fetched proposition. It is simply a challenge to jettison everything that holds you back, then catapult your awareness into regions that remain unimaginable for most. *Flow* is a dance with potential. It is the quintessential ingredient of *being*, which sets the stage for freedom.

From a Toltec perspective, *being* waits for us at the edges of the person of knowledge stage. In my opinion, once you learn to face potential, the only difference between you and don Juan is the level of skill. His ability to handle potential is immense, and this is what bestows upon him his abilities. That is, his skills result from his predilections, from following his path with heart. His path has become a direct expression of this core. Whatever occurs as a result of this dynamic is an effect of his natural evolution, which results from the intersection of his cohesion and Spirit. Put another way, *being* is a natural effect of continually tracking potential, staying in touch with it and allowing that connection to pull the best out of you.

Being results from fully activating body knowledge; the cornerstones of perception are all operational, and each is transcended into a unified whole that then establishes a unique relation with the world. *Being* is a state of on-going renewal, of continual discovery. *Being* liberates you from all form, and therefore delivers the experience of living rather than mentally recollecting bits and pieces of your life.

Being is also residing in the moment, and for this timing is essential. Timing in this sense means you have keen awareness of your place in the world, and how to navigate through it. As such, your refined balance with the world automatically leads you to optimal experiences. After all, there are enough anecdotes in metaphysical literature to prove that a natural path leads to a stronger, more peaceful life. Timing, therefore, stems from the moment, allows you to connect directly with the world, and promotes quality of life. To derive survival value from *being*, it must facilitate survival. Otherwise, what's the point? I trust you agree that having good health and abundant quality in your life are survival-related.

To have timing, you must gain masterful control of your energy body. Hence, proficiency with timing rests in the person of knowledge stage. That's when you've gone past form, including the forms of ordinary and nonordinary realities. You've also connected your energy body with the greater rhythms of Spirit. To do this you must become proficient with the related tracking skills of letting go, fluidity, nonattachment, accepting your fate, inaccessibility, and personal responsibility.

As a person of knowledge, you can step away from the familiar, connect with potential, and step moment by moment into the void. To make a good go of it, your instincts must be sharp. You must be able to sense how to behave within the moment, and from this awareness have your livelihood cared for. Otherwise, it's a quick spiral down into the dregs of existence. Fortunately, we have the accounts of don Juan and others that indicate that such a radical proposition is not only possible but feasible.

Being and Becoming

Being is an effect, a derivative of a person's lifelong work to bring himself to life. The stages of personal evolution, then, are steps to awaken the energy body, a process that delivers you to life. As you travel through the stages, the active ingredient of *being* is found in *becoming*, which is the motion of manifesting. Accordingly, *becoming* is developed through intent. As you intend to become a person of knowledge, for example, you're hooking into an end result, a goal. The ranger's waiting drill for manifesting (knowing that you're waiting, and what you're waiting for) embodies both *being* and *becoming*. Waiting is a posture of *being*; knowing what you're waiting for is a posture of *becoming*.

Like other ingredients on the Toltec path, this combination carries power, yet evaporates under scrutiny. If you define it, you're exercising self-importance. If you tell yourself what you are, if you identify yourself as being something (like an artist or a businessperson or a Toltec), then you remain isolated in that static energy of self-importance. In like manner, if you identify features of the path and world, such as *being* and *becoming*, you again pin perception to the definition, to the thoughts. In so doing, you remove yourself from *flow*, from *becoming*, from awakening completely, from the actual energy of a person of knowledge.

To stabilize the intent of a person of knowledge, self-importance must go. Body knowledge must rule. For, as don Juan says, a person of knowledge doesn't think (*Separate*, 114). A person of knowledge has cleaned her bubble of perception so well that there's no reflection, no internal dialogue. There's only awareness of the immediacy of the moment.

Therefore, keep in mind that the more you try to do something, anything, the less you are aware of other aspects of life. Therefore, let your path generate focus, momentum, and balance. Then step out of your way and let it all occur. Remain nonattached, even to your very own behavior. Just don't use this as an excuse to become a petty tyrant.

Becoming is the ability to track the movement of *being*, to move with life's experiences. Saturating yourself in each moment while letting completely go of each moment, allows your dream to change while maintaining a stable dream. Whether it is the dream of daily life, or dreaming other worlds, the process is the same.

Furthermore, as you familiarize yourself with *becoming*, you automatically begin to look into the face of time, to approach time as a current of energy. This movement originates in potential. To experience it directly, you must maneuver your cohesion to a new position. You must face upriver, so to speak, to witness the origins of time. You must also know how to navigate while traveling with this force, up or down river. Hence, the process and mastery of *flow*.

This dynamic process enables you to consolidate your life, including setting the stage for the future, while remaining steadfastly in the present. Typically, we measure our steps governed by what has occurred in the past. We reconstruct events, and by this assessment, manage our lives. Now, I'm not suggesting that you forget your experiences, and render them meaningless. I'm asking you to use them in another way. By gaining experience to beef up your energy body, and to generate more personal power, you gain the option of connecting face-to-face with the world. When you do, your experiences are in front of you, literally in your face. To perceive this requires awareness of having new options. Managing your life so that you tune yourself to optimal experiences requires body knowledge. And when you have enough knowledge about how to use your body, you activate *will*. Doing so is realizing your first significant step toward *being*.

Being, Will, and Intent

Through proficiency with the stages of evolution, you activate and manage *will*. Remember, *will* is the governing force of cohesion. It is the embodiment of body knowledge. To get to *will*, you have to step outside your thoughts . . . all of them. You must tap capacities of yourself that provide all the sense that thinking provides, plus more. You can't cut off your thoughts and hope everything will come out just fine and dandy. If you arbitrarily left thinking behind without another form of guidance, you'd be rudderless in a stormy sea. The channel markers of the stages allow you to form a new relation with the world gradually, steadily, and surely. To load the chances in favor of success, your venture must be done consciously, not randomly.

Indeed, Czikszentmihalyi says that consciousness is "intentionally ordered information."[3] Order arises from a stable cohesion. For our purposes, we need to expand the definition of "order" to include all kinds of data, not just verbal information. We need to ensure we're dealing with awareness that exists as a result of thinking as well as anything that exists outside of it. Now, to supplant the order of ordinary reality with the order of a nonordinary reality requires work, effort. This is what all the tracking exercises are for: to stimulate the work of it. To head off toward having a natural field requires even that much more work.

Czikszentmihalyi also says that intention (intent) is the force that maintains order.[4] In his own way, he describes the stable intent of *being* and the intent of movement, of growth, found in *becoming*. By relaxing into this pair, and by remaining vigilant to the work, you bring both to life. You *become* conscious. In so doing, you have brought yourself to life in a most remarkable and intelligent manner. For if you have the ability to manage your life, to generate positive experiences, to keep growing in leaps and bounds, and all the while have your awareness flooded with life each and every moment, then I submit to you that you are an evolved human being. You have become more intelligent than those who cannot perform the magic of being alive. And know that the potential for this intelligence resides within each and every one of us.

Will, then, is the application of this magic. It keeps cohesion together, keeps awareness ordered, and maintains your life. By the time you get here, you're well beyond ordinary meaning. For, as don Juan says, his *will* is what keeps him alive regardless of his personal choice, or regardless of anything he *sees* about the world (*Separate*, 106). He has let go to that degree. As a result, he is part of the magic of Spirit. After all, it's really the magic of Spirit that delivers the evolution, the greater intelligence, not human folly.

Being and Evolution

Arriving at *being* requires having a precision life. In the film *Apollo 13*, astronauts returning from the moon had a disabled spacecraft. Based on the true story of NASA's Apollo 13 trek into space, oxygen tanks ruptured, electrical systems failed, and the astronauts were truly put to the test. In order to re-enter Earth's atmosphere safely, they had to navigate their craft within a paper-thin margin. To do otherwise would have them bounce off Earth's atmosphere like a billiard ball, and speed through space to meet their certain doom. Likewise, traveling the trajectory of freedom requires hitting a paper-thin margin. The odds are staggering, but don Juan and others have hit the margin. This means there's at least a little room for us to navigate the path to freedom, also.

Accordingly, here are a few applications of tracking skills that may help you engage astronaut-level training.

Flow. *Flow* is a mastery of time, space, and cohesion. Therefore, push yourself beyond your limits and into new relationships with the world. Tackle the unknown. Consolidate the known. Since the goal is to live with Spirit, let Spirit flow through you and direct your steps. Give the dream of daily life its freedom. Let freedom come to you. If you force the world into compliance with your thoughts, you don't stand a chance of getting to your core. Manipulation is in the domain of petty tyrants.

Flow is a relaxed state. Relaxation, remember, is your ticket to a natural energy field. Having a natural field is not something that can be forced; it is not plowed with conditional energy. There is no ordinary definition to it, so you don't have to force an issue to maintain it. Residing in a natural field is maintaining *flow*.

Human First. *Being* is necessary to arrive at freedom. It characterizes the person of knowledge, which means it sets the stage for an evolution beyond the human condition. But being human is an essential ingredient to enact this evolution. You have a body, and it's a human one to boot. Therefore, being a ranger is about peaking the human experience.

Now the whole gig of being human, according to don Juan, is that we are luminous creatures. As such, our natural function is that of being aware, of perceiving. Indeed, don Juan takes this to a grand height when he says, "We are not objects; we have no solidity. We are boundless." Accordingly, he says that experiencing the world as material is a play of mind to make our passage on Earth convenient. He adds that it is when we get lost in reason that we develop difficulties (*Tales*, 100).

Because "we are boundless," the world must be as well. We try to contain it, however, through all of our thinking about it. All theories, all worldviews, all conditional energy fields, all philosophies, all religions are based in reason.

They are formulations about the world; they are not the world itself. As such, they have form, which is the hallmark of reason. When you tackle potential, you tackle formlessness. Being able to remain levelheaded while in a free-flow universe is done through *will*; more appropriately, through having a well-developed *will*. This requires the right and left sides of the energy body to strike a harmony. This is what tracking and dreaming provide, as it is also a function of Hemi-Sync™. Systems can deliver results.

But this is also the catch. When you work with a system, you work with form. You then increase the odds of losing yourself in this work rather than breaking free. Losing yourself in this way results in fundamentalist thinking. Fortunately, the modern-cycle Toltecs accounted for this when they revamped their philosophy. In the chapter "Straight from the Heart" we take a close look at fundamentalism, especially the metaphysical variety.

One way "human first" plays itself out is this: Say you're a businessperson, but your primary program is to be a Toltec. As a result, you make your business (or your art, craft, or whatever) an expression of what Victor Sanchez calls *Toltequity*, which is the life and essence of Toltec philosophy.[5] By doing so, you let your primary program of personal evolution have precedence over just making a living. Because you don't want to get lost in the system, though, you incorporate into your programs that you're first a human, a perceiver. In relation to this, your Toltec studies are a secondary program because what you really want to do is learn to perceive better, to become more aware. Toltec studies are just a method to do this. With this relationship of priorities, you set the stage to manage all these powerful influences. To accent the purpose of perceiving, rather than just becoming a Toltec, don Juan teaches not to believe in anything, other than that the world is mysterious (*Tales,* ch. 4).

Path with Heart. Your path is not only what you give your life to, it's what brings you life. It's an energy line that connects you with your core. Thus, it's what connects you with *flow*. A path with heart is continually unfolding, ever changing. Yet it delivers a constancy that enables you to connect with potential, the crucial element of *being*. By remaining with potential, you stand a chance of elevating your life to its highest potential: freedom. Just remember to intend positive results. Otherwise, you become an expert at manifesting the unusual and the bizarre, but never really get anywhere.

Petty Tyrant. Petty tyrants can help you learn freedom, or how to endure pain. I recommend the former.

A petty tyrant exerts pressure on the energy body from outside the bubble. This requires an internal shift to meet and exceed this energy, the internal shift being a shift in cohesion. This is why Toltecs can't get enough of these cosmic bullies. Petty tyrants ensure you have plenty of practice in shifting and stabilizing cohesions. Get enough of their nonsense and the work required to taste freedom begins to make sense.

This doesn't mean you must be a passive dishrag. There comes a time when you have to stand up for yourself. Before this magic moment arrives, though, you should be able to parry most of your petty tyrant's maneuvers to control you. Otherwise, while you may not fall off the tuna boat, you're going to miss its departure. So don't miss the boat. Put in the work—and I do mean work—to track yourself. The essence of it is that your reactions originate from your karma, not the petty tyrant's. Therefore, each time you are thrown off the mark by a petty tyrant, recapitulate the event to track your projection, and your self-importance.

Then parlay your efforts into management of your energy body. Use the external pressure to step aside from petty influences and aim for your core. Tons of pressure turns coal into diamonds. The more you discover yourself being unaffected by the onslaughts of the less advantaged, the more you'll silently rejoice in your evolution.

You may also use petty tyrants to work your way through your chakras. For example, when petty tyrants push emotional buttons, don't suppress your energies, but don't fly off the handle, either. In order words, one of your goals is to not let the situation get the best of you. Otherwise, you place undue strain on your body. In this example, by not managing your emotions, you interfere with the flow of energy up your chakra system. You then distort first-chakra energies, those related to your physical body. This leads to further distortions of your second-chakra energies, your emotions. Plus, by interpreting the petty tyrant as a moron, you distort the third chakra, your intellect, by the way you think.

Continuing up the ladder, speaking calmly promotes the flow of energy to the fifth chakra; stepping away from the turmoil of petty tyrants and into dreaming eases energy into the sixth chakra; and remaining true to your primary program lets energy fully enter the seventh chakra.

A positive relationship with your energy body stimulates a harmonious flow of energy throughout the entire chakra system, and thereby energizes the entire energy body. An even, well-regulated flow is an optimum state for you to produce results while generating the least amount of energy loss. *Being* is having attained expert-level status with this process.

Your struggle with petty tyrants is magnified if you seek retribution. If you do, you're letting the situation get the best of you. You're also becoming a petty tyrant. Remember the idea is to learn nonattachment, how to let go and remain unaffected, and figure out how to remain focused in the heat of battle. To do this, you must behave from the reference of a larger pattern. When all else fails, choose chaos.

Recapitulation. Recapitulating your energy body, from surface to core and back again, is what occurs when you recapitulate your entire life's experiences. As you do, you work through the karma of a multitude of cohesions. As you discharge energy, you automatically learn to better manage your energy body. And, as a result, you come into *being*.

Self-Importance. Remember what self-importance is: self-enhancement and self-reflection. So stop kicking yourself in the butt—stop brooding. That's the self-enhancement part.

Thinking is the self-reflection part. As a result, you get to stop telling yourself what the world is like, and get comfortable with not knowing anything. Especially don't tell yourself what the Toltec world is like. If you do, you're a goner. The system is for liberation, not making a dictionary. Tracking builds and fortifies the foundation to follow an evolutionary path, and dreaming delivers the expansion, the *becoming* of it. Together they deliver *being*, the complete realization, as well as the pure understanding of it.

This type of transformation is not a matter of talk. You have to live it, breathe it. Remember, a person of knowledge doesn't think. He *is*. If you haven't completely stabilized a stage of growth, then you're not there. You may reflect on it, interpret your world based on it, talk all day long about it, but fluency with your intellect doesn't mean you can actually do anything.

Until you've reached the person of knowledge stage, every perception—*everything*—is a matter of projection. As you progress, you clean the mirrors of your bubble of perception. The trick is to polish away until they become translucent, until your light passes through them to connect with the emanations. You then *become* light. It's not like you aren't already light; but the process of remembering is full of deception, as we think we've remembered our nature when we haven't.

You automatically, and with an ironclad guarantee, limit your connections with potential by your thoughts and feelings of how you fit into the world. Busting loose of the karma to let yourself realize this connection is the work of it, the pure understanding of it.

Living in infinite potential means you also live in a universe of infinite realities. Remember, the world and you are boundless. Therefore, losing self-importance equates with gaining more awareness. The goal, after all, is to become totally aware.

Parallel Realities

After several sessions with ETs in TMI's lab, I grew a little bored. I longed for something more compelling. As I walked into the lab one afternoon, I noticed a tape teetering on the edge of a shelf. It was the 1.5-hertz binaural beat tape mentioned in the last chapter.

The monitors graciously accepted my request to experiment with the tape, and everything went like clockwork. They hooked me up to physiological monitoring devices and closed the door to the "black box." Like a float tank, the booth shuts out all light and most noise. This sensory deprivation frees up energy that might otherwise be used to pay attention to physical perceptions.

As soon as I centered myself in the tones, I found myself flying down a tunnel toward white light. Having recently seen the film *Poltergeist*, I was full of apprehension. I remembered a scene where a psychic is trying to retrieve a little girl. The psychic is worried that the girl will pass through the other world into the white light and never be found again. With this remembrance, I found myself silently yelling, "Don't let me go into the white light, you'll never get me back!" I then forced myself to exit the tunnel, and went around to the opposite side of a magnificent, huge ball of light. Once there, I *saw* another world. It was just like the one I was familiar with only everything was reversed in a mirror-image fashion.

The next day, I had another lab session. We used the same binaural beat. This time I didn't go through a tunnel. I went straight to the light. Adhering to my discipline of fighting fear, I dove in. I felt, *saw*, remembered . . . a universe made up of pure potential. In the midst of this potential was an infinite number of realities. In one reality, the only difference between this one and that one was that one hair on my girlfriend's head was different. Since there was one variation, the entire world was different. This extrapolated so that I *saw* a world where I was the monitor, not the subject, of the lab session, another where I never had heard of TMI, another where I wasn't born to this world, on and on and on. I also knew that whichever reality was experienced by any individual was a matter of intent, of focus, of karmic cohesion.

This session was years ago. To this date, I have never lost sense of the magnitude of a boundless world. Indeed, dreaming and *seeing* have elevated it from a point of awareness to a point of knowledge.

Earth Changes

Applying this notion of parallel realities to a common metaphysical topic, let's look at *earth changes* for a moment. The subject of *earth changes* generally involves talk about Earth evolving through some kind of change. For some, Earth is on the brink of major geological cataclysms. For others, humans are catching on to a grander philosophical scheme and are changing at fundamental levels. Of course, there's a multitude of combinations in and around *earth changes* thinking. From an infinite-potential, parallel-reality perspective, all variations of human and

Earth evolution are occurring. What's more, as learned from our brief foray into time, they're all happening right now; or in the past or future, depending—depending on where you're focused, where your focal point is, what pattern of energy dominates your energy body.

As reported in a major newspaper, scientific findings indicate a "colossal shift in the Earth's mass half a billion years ago," which may account for great shifts in continents and a general enhancement of evolution.[6] So there is information out there that says cataclysms occur. Hence, they might occur again. On a lesser scale of disaster, but equally dramatic, is how science and history are revised, or evolve, depending on your perspective. A brief look at history shows us that one scientific theory after another has been revised. Where once Earth was the center of the universe, now it's just a speck resting in an immensity of space. In concert with this, have you ever noticed how one historical fact after another falls away? Dating the oldest known human remains, for example, edges its way further back in time the more anthropologists explore and discover. History changes.

We live in a free-flow world, but we try to hold on to a fixed pattern with all our might. This is why it's important to let go. Otherwise, your projections may create cataclysms in your life. If you want to evolve, and you hold on to your patterns, Spirit will shift a few things for you.

I've noticed at least four patterns associated with *earth changes*. The first is that at some point just about everyone who gets into metaphysics takes an *earth changes* course. It seems to be required. In it, people talk about how things are changing, how good and evil seem to be polarizing, how the world will tilt on its axis, and how all hell will break loose. This is the first pattern. The second pattern is that these people tend to regard themselves as the new leaders of humanity once the changes occur. Some even start rooting for the changes to occur, as though such violent upheaval were a sporting contest. Not only is this self-importance, but their lives must be a bunch of slush to desire carnage.

The third pattern is that the people who cling to their thoughts about major upheaval soon experience it. Their businesses go bust. Their relationships fall violently apart. Their emotions constantly tear them up inside; and illness often results. From a manifesting model, their mind-set produces the results they focus on. The fourth pattern is that people gradually begin to see that the violence doesn't have to occur, that it's projection, that there are other options, other ways to manage and focus energy. For example, they realize that if enough people learn meditation, and calm down, this will prevent violent changes in the environment. Thus, any internal changes become mirrored externally.

My pet hypothesis is that, since a person's cohesion begins to shift once placed in a metaphysical arena, this change is projected outward as *earth changes*. The microcosm pushed off to the macrocosm. The balance of the matter is to not buy in to the thinking that violent change must occur, while not ignoring news that suggests severe *earth changes* may occur, or are occurring. Holding on to pet theories can be dangerous. After all, not paying attention to all the information led to the demise of the Toltec civilization. Then again, perhaps an even more refined balance is to track the topic even further.

Following these lines of thought, we come back to the awareness of infinite, parallel realities. Which one will you experience? All of them, one way or another. If land masses shift, and we're thrown into the dark ages, then you and your friends will simultaneously live and die. On Earth X-90425, for instance, you live through the changes. But on Earth X-90436, you die from them. On Earth X-80011, your friends think you're alive, but the you that you know in this life is on Earth X-90425. From your current perspective, you're not with your friends, but from the perspective of an energy line emanating from the you in this life, you and your friends are trying to make a good go of it on Earth X-80011.

So what's the point? What's the deal? The deal of the cards is your fate. It's where you are right here, right now. It's the sum total of your karma. It's how Spirit is experiencing its own creation. It's living in the midst of infinite potential.

13

GUIDANCE SYSTEMS

Manifesting, or bringing something into awareness, and having it remain stable and usable, occurs from the interaction between form and potential. Form is cohesion, a type of energy field. Potential is abstract energy; that is, energy that has possibilities of realization but isn't there yet. Pure potential is completely abstract, the infinite creation that contains everything. How these two energies play together determines what is realized, or manifested. Remember that whatever is realized directly reflects your cohesion, or what pattern of energy you've stabilized. It also governs how you continue to connect with potential, which governs what you'll manifest next. So you have the energy body meeting greater emanations. This meeting produces a dance between potential and realization: the disco of manifesting, the burning off of karma, the navigation of infinite potential.

If you're not hooking up with potential, you're just circling within the conditional field you already have. This may keep you amused, but you're not going to grow too much. Plus, when you face squarely with potential, you're placing your life squarely on the line, each and every moment. Using death as an adviser, nonattachment, and inaccessibility all helped you get to this magic place. To stay there, you need to elevate your skill in using all the basic exercises. Doing so removes you from talk about life, and into a relationship with the world where you are living it to the hilt.

An ongoing personal transformation occurs when you apply your manifesting skills to the stages of evolution. By now, you should have a grasp of this journey, a sense of what game is afoot. Having this sense is crucial to stay in the game. But, in and of itself, it's not enough to withstand the daily rigors of navigating a metaphysical path. Since it's not all that difficult to be thrown off the tuna boat, let's look at perspectives and skills—navigational aids—that will help you sail into freedom.

Perhaps the most difficult part of learning guidance is cutting yourself loose from all your concerns in order to be aware of the promptings of Spirit. Spirit speaks in many languages, and comes in many forms. You might feel a soft, inner voice, or have a traffic sign—an omen—placed directly in front of you. When you give yourself permission to be guided by Spirit, you're tapping higher orders of awareness. Therefore, a request from Spirit for seemingly nonsensical behavior usually turns out to be quite brilliant after the dust settles. Spirit has a full sense of the entire playing field, not just the position you're playing.

Let's first tackle inner guidance, then move on to outer forms. At some point, these distinctions become meaning less. As you transform yourself, everything in your life, including all that you perceive and experience, becomes part of "you."

Inner Guidance

In some way, shape, or form all guidance hinges on body knowledge. As such, all require paying attention to what the body senses, and to how you relate to any given event; in other words, listening. Since we're first addressing inner guidance, let's place listening in terms of the energy body's innate modes of perception, the cornerstones: dreaming, feeling, *seeing*, and *will*.

Dreaming. Some people say that you must have the same dream a number of times for it to be considered revelatory or meaningful. From personal experience, dreams that repeat themselves usually mean something is at work, and the message within the dream is begging for attention. At the same time, while a one-time-only, very vivid dream might be the result of too much pizza, such a dream might carry enough weight by itself to be considered as holding portent, as signaling bona fide guidance.

The way to figure out which is which is to educate your intuition. Sense what a dream tells you. Does your body tell you your interpretation feels right? Plus, recapitulate the dream to discover its meaning. Did you eat too much, or does it carry a prophetic note? This helps you figure out your feelings that much better.

You may also set up dreaming to find specific guidance. Carry a question into dreaming, for example, and let your dream play itself out. Pay attention to the images, and to how you feel. Don't censor your dream. Give yourself plenty of room to experience whatever—and I mean whatever—unfolds in the dream. Anything can happen in a dream, and usually does; after all, you're in dreamland. Typically, though, a dream settles down once the energies behind it discharge. So if a dream is violent, it may turn peaceful if you don't repress the images. Let it work itself out and discover where it takes you.

You may also apply this as an exercise of stretching out your *will*, a playing-with-death exercise. To do so, enter the blackness of level-one dreaming, then let your awareness disperse, ooze, or flow far into the dream. Then let your energies be at rest. Next, observe your energies returning, consolidating within your physical body. This reorganization occurs when your *will* is ready to let it occur.

As you work with dreaming, you may become a little starry-eyed, or want to hug everyone because you have so much love bouncing around inside. From this point, you might get a little too pie-in-the-sky. Just remember that you need ruthlessness, and you need to remain grounded to get on with the program, which includes accurate guidance. To better use dreaming, observe yourself, remain nonattached and fluid, and assume personal responsibility for all your actions.

Feeling. Realizations stemming from emotional outbursts are fleeting, says don Juan (*Fire*, 278–279). This means that when you click on insights that are packed with emotion, they tend to be of very limited value, and don't withstand the test of time. Hence the need for educating our emotions, our feelings, our intuition. In this way, we cultivate the feeling cornerstone as a viable method of guidance.

Intuition, an aspect of feeling, is a full-bodied, multidimensional form of guidance. It's full-bodied in that it requires body knowledge. It relies on being fully aware of how you're feeling. For that, you need your body. It's funny that way. It's multidimensional in that at some level, conscious or not, you're aware of different dimensions, and are connected with various modes of perception.

Feeling is like a collection house. It gathers, or is connected with, many influences, then delivers appropriate insights at appropriate times. Feeling may even be thought of as having tentacles extending throughout regions of consciousness, such as the regions that chaos theory deals with. As a result, you're aware of irregular, or unknown, patterns in the universe, as well as regular, or ordinary, patterns within your known world. This means you can be intuitively aware of something without a rational foundation to explain why. As you can imagine, managing such complex behavior requires rigorous education.

Applying feeling to work in your life requires listening to gentle nudges, and ever-so-soft feelings. If you don't, all heck may break loose. Not that it will, but one little thing not in place may produce very large ramifications. That is, if you overlook even a tiny form of guidance you may experience catastrophic results. For example, a Toltec I know was having her silver-mercury dental fillings replaced with quartz-based composite fillings. She did so to remove the toxic substance from her mouth. Just before entering the dentist's office, she felt a twinge to have only one large filling replaced on that day. Eager to get the procedure finished, she had all fillings replaced. However, a large replacement filling was not formed exactly like the previous one. This threw her entire bite off, requiring numerous trips to the dentist to restore a proper alignment of her teeth. While the dentist did own up to making a mistake, she assumed complete responsibility, realizing that if she had been more patient, and listened to her guidance, the difficulty would not have occurred. With only one filling to concern himself, the dentist would have remembered the exact size of the filling to be replaced. As a result, contrary to the popular method of filing a malpractice lawsuit, she used her guidance to help the dentist restore her bite. Before she continued with him, however, she set up an omen to see if she should stay with him. Receiving a favorable indication, they set about the task of restoration. By the way, she says her body felt better as soon as the mercury was removed.

I'm sure you can recognize something similar. How many times have you felt like behaving one way, only to behave according to your habits, or according to your personal thoughts or wishes? Then, later, it dawns on you that you should have acted differently.

Seeing. *Seeing* is like peering through something, through outer manifestations into deeper, root energies. This makes it a marvelous technique for guidance. Like any skill, it requires training to develop. Don Juan says that at first *seeing* carries many distortions, making it difficult to figure out and use. Later, it becomes a direct link with intent, a direct way of knowing (*Tales,* 154). Keep in mind that its visual nature may be misleading. *Seeing* hinges on connecting, or merging, the entire body with what is being *seen*. It's not something that's done just with the eyes.

In general, guidance reveals itself in many ways. *Seeing* is no different. You might experience a bundle of energy that leaves you with a knowing. You might have a vision, or simply perceive a mental image. A response to your request for guidance might come as a voice, a silent voice that really isn't anywhere. In each case, it's a matter of establishing an intent for guidance, then getting out of your way to perceive an answer. Using *seeing* for guidance is much like obtaining guidance while dreaming. But, since *seeing* tends to be a more direct method, you become instantly aware rather than having to decode or interpret a dream.

As you develop your *seeing*, you learn to discriminate among images, body sensations, and voices, learning what to trust, what you can bank your life on. To begin, start with questions that aren't very complicated. Should you eat a hot dog? Should you take a day off from work? While these are simple enough, keep in mind that however you act carries weight. The smallest decision in your life could create the greatest effects. So be responsible. Pay attention. Experiment.

Will. Here is body knowledge at its finest. With *will*, you consolidate the other cornerstones of perception simultaneously. You then receive promptings from Spirit in different ways at different times, since activating *will* means you have developed to some degree the skill of tapping the cornerstones. Also, with *will* you're centered in your body. Therefore, you're able to pay attention better, to respond better to unfolding events, and to learn better from your experiences.

Keep in mind that you're changing cohesions all the time as you evolve. As a result, when you feel prompted to "go buy a beer" it might be the result of your old habits, an old cohesion. If you make up your mind not to drink alcohol, stick with your decision. Doing so causes your cohesion to shift and stabilize that much faster. You don't have time to be fooling around.

In addition to *will*, *seeing*, feeling, and dreaming are all done with the body. Therefore, the more you practice using the cornerstones the more you're developing body knowledge. Conversely, the more you develop body knowledge, the more you'll command the cornerstones.

Outer Guidance

Seems like people have a tendency to look outside of themselves for answers, blindly follow authority, and relinquish personal responsibility. Well, the flip side is that tapping external guidance can take you outside your normal frame of reference. This is a good thing. Anytime we break through the walls that confine perception, we've done well. In addition, Csikszentmihalyi says that good feedback helps navigate awareness into *flow*.[1] Feedback often comes from external reference points. At the same time, giving our decision making over to the dictums of a board game, to dead people (just because they're dead doesn't mean they're right), to some Atlantean master in another realm who speaks through the earthbound living, is really asking too much. With all this in mind, let's poke around outer forms of guidance.

Cognitive Guidance. Cognitive guidance is made up of the mental influences that govern our behavior. For instance, in *Emotional Intelligence,* Goleman makes the point that uncontrolled anger results from a lack of cognitive guidance. He says it's an inability to control base-level emotions through the application of reason.[2] He also indicates that many of our emotional memories that have evolved over thousands of years may be out of date, "especially in the fluid social world we humans inhabit."[3] If so, these emotional guideposts generate behavior that hasn't kept pace with the world we've built. In short, our guidance systems need overhaul. As a result, we're out of touch, and out of balance.

Thought focuses energy. In fact, Goleman points out that thought is a major influence in determining what emotions are experienced.[4] In addition, thought is so powerful it produces entire worldviews, entire realities. But, again, these are only intellectual constructions. Now, we've covered how the intellect is only a slice of the pie, whereas the body is connected with the entire pie. We've also covered the interplay between thought and emotion. Let's use these to explore the guiding influences of worldviews a little more.

For our purposes here, cognitive guidance is also a highfalutin term for the predetermined guidance a metaphysical system offers. Keep in mind that a philosophy contains a worldview and techniques that bring the worldview to life. From a Toltec perspective, "Spirit" is part of the worldview, and altering routines, nonattachment, and becoming accessible to Spirit are a few techniques that help bring Spirit to life. Even on a scale of simply educating our emotions, Toltec exercises of altering routines and nonattachment interrupt ordinary behavior. This intervention allows new behaviors to come to life, thereby helping us adapt to "the fluid social world."

A system contains procedures, tips on how to realize your goals. But these exercises that are intended to awaken you may be deceptive. For example, erasing personal history is not just to camouflage yourself. While this effect is in play (you don't want to be placed in a box by people's thoughts about you), it's principally a means to dislodge the focal point. This automatically occurs when you no longer maintain a specific continuity of your thoughts; that is, when you no longer regard yourself as being the same person day in and day out. If you talk about yourself in different ways, you eventually *see* yourself in different ways. As a result, you're not trying to bolster the image you have of yourself. This is also part of losing self-importance. The effect is that you loosen cohesion, which then lets you awaken your energy body. If you erase personal history only for the disguise of it, you miss the point.

The problem is that since a metaphysical guidance system accounts for so much, it can be quite intimidating. In fact, a good system can account for anything you experience. What's the problem, then? The problem is that you might lose yourself in the gyroscope and not sail the ocean in front of you. To avoid this danger, a good guidance system teaches you guidance, period, not dogma. That is, a viable system portrays its teachings as a form of guidance, not as a completely accurate picture of reality. As a result, when you aim your intent toward freedom, your guidance keeps you on track. By so doing, you develop your own guidance system. You learn how to think for yourself, which transforms outer guidance into inner guidance. When you learn this, you're on your way to activating *will*, which delivers an even more powerful form of guidance.

As don Juan says, a rationalization is just a position of the focal point, an alignment, a cohesion (*Fire,* 278). This may be expanded to say that a worldview is a focal point position reflecting a very intense cohesion. To step out of one worldview into another, and then into freedom, you must expertly manage your energy body. This is the point of metaphysical training.

Omens. Omens, or signs, have been around a long, long time. Julian Jaynes, for example, explores many varieties of omens in his book, *The Origin of Consciousness in the Breakdown of the Bicameral Mind*.[5] From comet trails to cloud formations to eclipses, from facial characteristics to dreams to hallucinations, omens have always been part and parcel of human behavior. There is no doubt they are a key element in a Toltec's lifestyle.

Indeed, until you get a good handle on intuition and *seeing*, omens serve as an excellent bridge to understanding the communications of Spirit. Plus, until you establish a firm direction in your life, they also help guide you through the random influences that push and pull at you when you first enter formlessness.

In a manner, omens are like the signposts found in dreaming. By serving as external reference points, they help take you out of your normal habits. Indeed, they help elevate perception into heightened awareness, or dreaming-while-awake. That is, they help transform your ordinary feel of the world into the perception that daily life is a type of dream.

Omens also help you figure out internal guidance because intuition is a key to deciphering them. When you witness an omen, for example, don't tell yourself what just occurred. Nonpattern it. Then ask yourself what it means, and wait for an intuitive reply. Make sure you don't bend an interpretation to suit your personal desires. As you build up your omen vocabulary, you'll recognize some omens immediately. Others will be filed for future reference. You'll have to wait and watch how your life unfolds, then match the omen on file with whatever occurs. You may start building this language by determining your positive and negative colors, your "yes" and "no" omens.

For example, during a recent trip to London, my companion and I were walking about town as I explained omens to her. Since she wanted to give it a go, I asked Spirit to show us what her positive color would be for the day. I told her she could change it later, but for practical purposes we needed references for that afternoon. As I asked, a red automobile pulled up to the curb and stopped in front of us. Okay, red it was. I then asked for her negative color. A white taxi turned from another street in front of us. Now, part of the omen was that these events were out of the ordinary. We had not seen any red cars stop in front of us, nor had I seen too many white cabs that day. They stood out, which is part of what omens are all about.

So there we were, boppin' about town having a great time reading omens. Then we decided to eat. She was not familiar with the area, so she wanted to turn left and head back to where she knew the turf. I said let's use omens, instead. After all, that was the curriculum for the day. As soon as she agreed, a red car passed us heading in the opposite direction than she initially wanted to go. We turned around and followed. Walking three blocks, a woman dressed in black stopped, bent over, and adjusted her shoe. To me, black means death, which means the event gets an exclamation point. Black is neither good nor bad; it means pay greater attention. Then we noticed a white car parked just past the woman. We stopped. Immediately to our right was a pub. I asked if this is where we should eat, and a man wearing a red shirt walked inside. We followed.

I had been hungry for a traditional English meal of roast and vegetables. It turned out that this was the pub's evening special. My friend had fish and chips, which she raved about, saying the pub was a true find and she had to return. Case closed.

Other times, when the meaning is not so readily apparent, you should ask Spirit what the omen means. You'll then receive inner guidance, or perhaps another omen will pop up in front of you.

Other symbols you might want to develop are road kills when you're on the highway, the behavior of birds, messages on billboards, what someone says at just the right moment, or what kind of book falls off a shelf in front of you. For instance, a friend of mine uses highway road kills to indicate that trouble looms ahead. I also use them as a way for death to speak to me, but in a different way. When I notice a road kill, I let the energy surrounding the dead animal shift its body into some type of message. I might then *see* a dead squirrel's body change into a sleeping posture that facilitates dreaming. I know it's related to dreaming because of the intuitive guidance that accompanies the change in the animal's form.

In the same manner, words on billboards might change, literally. So when others are reading an ordinary advertisement, you could be reading a message from Spirit. These forms of guidance require a solid balance with the world. Otherwise, there are too many distortions.

At any rate, you can decipher omens from virtually anything. An omen might be the same for several people, or it might mean several different things. Whatever the case, it's up to you to figure out your agreements with Spirit to create your personal omen dictionary. This may sound nuts to some, I know, but Spirit communicates with us all the time. Think of the wonder of that!

Here are two more examples just to give you an idea of how fun all this is. The first occurred years ago, when Halley's comet was passing by. Even with all the media hullabaloo, I had not been paying too much attention to this cosmic wonder. The morning it passed closest to Earth, though, I found the rear window of my automobile had been shot with a pellet gun. A small hole was surrounded by shattered glass that formed what looked like a comet and its tail. I asked what this meant and the silent answer was "Pay attention." I was too caught up in my own thoughts, in my own drama of living, and totally oblivious to stretching further into life.

The second example demonstrates the daily practicality of omens. A couple of years ago I received an invitation to travel to England to give a seminar on the material I write about. I had been off the lecture circuit for over a year, as I was burned out. I had traveled for over six years and the mere mention of a workshop made me nauseous. But this invitation felt good, and I hadn't been to Europe in a while. I had also spent the year recapitulating my prior experiences, which had the effect of restoring much of my balance, and making me more aware of how not to lose myself while teaching. But unsure of what was best, I set up an omen. I asked Spirit to show me a British flag next to my positive or negative color, depending on Spirit's wishes regarding giving the seminar. A couple of days later I parked my car on the far side of a post office's parking lot. I walked directly toward its doors. Right in front of the doors was a car painted in my positive color. On its rear bumper was a sticker of the British flag. I accepted the invitation, and had a great time. With subsequent visits, I have come to truly appreciate the fine ranger spirit found in Britain.

Spirit Guides. People have reported being influenced by entities on the "other side" for quite some time. Indeed, entire metaphysical movements, such as Spiritualism, have been based on being able to communicate with discarnate beings.

On a number of occasions over the years, for example, I have felt the presence of my deceased father. At times, it seems as though he renders some type of gentle guidance. Other times, it seems his influence saved the day, liberating me to continue my Toltec travels. To me, this is evidence suggestive that some form of life beyond death occurs. But there are other explanations that can account for the same events, without bringing in afterlife survival. These may be addressed in a future work. For now, I just want to touch base on the feasibility of guidance from the departed.

For instance, in recent years *channeling* has gained wide acceptance as a way to gather knowledge. Channeling occurs by releasing one's vocal cords to another entity. Trance channeling occurs when the person channeling completely removes his conscious influence, and the entity being channeled may even have the person up and about, walking and talking. An interesting shift in the focal point, this is.

But, as with most anything else, you should take care when entering the unknown. Don Juan, for instance, says that inhabitants of the inorganic world can create projections, images to entice wayfaring dreamers. This is not a dire situation. Remain on your toes, and know that perhaps there are more friendly inhabitants residing deeper in consciousness than those from the inorganic world. The point here is that a spirit guide might be none other than an inorganic being who is trying to make you feel so special that you'll relinquish your power to that realm. Don Juan says that that is what they do, try to make you feel like you have power. As a result, they only guide you into self-importance (*Dreaming,* 99, 177, 101).

While deliberately getting involved with these creatures may seem perverse, contact with them is a significant test of your resources. Because of its wild explorations, the Toltec Way is different from many metaphysical paths. Being tested helps keep balance and perspective. Plus, reason cannot withstand the jolt that dealing with the inorganic world delivers. Reason cannot fully handle such an experience; the idea of it, yes, the life of it, no. This makes reason loosen up, and then give way to body knowledge. Then again, maybe we've outgrown the need for the inorganic world. Maybe contact with ETs can deliver the same impact.

Another thing to consider is that even when the knowledge being channeled is high caliber, it might be harder for the channeler to live up to the knowledge coming through. Thus, personal evolution is at risk. Since the channeled information is removed from the channeler's immediate experience, it's always "out there," coming from another place. By contrast, dreaming levels require that a person thoroughly learn a stage before proceeding. Evolution is built into the structure. Therefore, it's easier to get a fix on personal responsibility. For example, learning to have OBEs requires you to get a handle on those dreaming energies. You need the personal experience of the knowledge. You must then engage dreaming to proceed.

At the same time, from experience channeling extraterrestrial intelligence, I know that channeling is a definite shift in the focal point, and is therefore another valuable experience in stimulating the energy body. Staying tuned to your primary program is what keeps you from being pinned down to the status quo. It lets you take the experience, and the information, and turn it all into knowledge.

The overriding idea, therefore, is that you should retain personal responsibility for each and every experience, whether you're working with dead masters or traveling the heights of dreaming.

$$\mathscr{D}\ \mathscr{D}\ \mathscr{D}$$

The crucial element in developing different forms of guidance, and allowing yourself to be guided, is losing self-importance. You must allow a higher power, a greater sense of awareness than your immediate knowledge, to guide your steps. This doesn't mean to forego what you know. That's also guidance. It means loosen up, stretch out, and connect with energies that are not part of your current known world.

To master guidance, you need to be in *flow*. To stay in *flow*, you have to let go. When you let go, you open yourself to many different influences. So you don't want to be random about the matter, doing just any ol' thing. Letting go to the extent of going on a beer binge, or getting those tattoos you never really wanted, isn't what I mean. You must retain purpose of mind and manner. This is where guidance comes in. It helps you move deliberately into new relationships with the world.

PART VII

THE
BALANCE
OF
EVOLUTION

14

IT'S
ONLY
NATURAL

As luminous-body perceivers, learning is what humans do naturally. From many educational perspectives, and certainly from a Toltec point of view, learning is measured by changes in behavior—be they intellectual, emotional, physical, psychic, or otherwise. The stages along a metaphysical path reflect multilevel changes, not only how and what you think, and how you look at the world, but how you participate with it as well. As you increase your learning skills, you evolve. Therefore, learning indicates an increased ability to do, to act.

In these terms, don Juan also taught Castaneda that a Toltec ranger is one who hunts knowledge (*Journey,* ch. 6). To be this kind of hunter requires the skill of self-motivated learning, which is the ability to track knowledge under your own head of steam, including where you fit in the natural order of things. From this relation comes a sense of security. For you either have security, or you don't. Money surely won't buy it; your skill as a hunter bestows it.

A good philosophy requires that you learn for mastery, that you fully engage self-motivated learning to become secure within your own right. The structure of a system is to help you get to the essence of your quest. Learning Toltec practices and views, for instance, supports stepping away from its structure to make a leap beyond its form; indeed, beyond all known boundary markers. To make this kind of leap requires a series of strong steps, with each step furthering your ability to learn. So this is where the levels of dreaming and the stages of evolution come in.

Each step requires that you enter into certain agreements with the world. To study astronomy, for instance, you have to agree that the world is round, that Earth revolves around the Sun, and that stars are a great distance away. In like manner, by studying the Toltec world, you agree that sophisticated dreaming practices exist, that the world is composed of energy, that you may communicate with Spirit, and that the universe contains many worlds—physical and nonphysical.

As you travel through Toltec worlds, for example, you might initially construct an agreement that elemental spirits exist. This helps you enter that terrain, then helps you expand that experience to participate more fully with the entire world as a living, intelligent presence. Later your interests might expand into nonordinary healing, which further helps you gain mastery over your resources. Still later you might use your agreements to build a life in another universe, which permits you to step outside the very learning that enabled your travels in the first place.

Difficulties with learning arise when you can't shift your energies. If you have a fixed-in-place cohesion, you can't entertain views that are not a part of that energy. There is no openness, no avenue for new information to register. At the same time, your energy should be stable. If it's not, you can't relate to new material. So be open, flexible, and yet very stable.

The formation of a watermark represents having integrated learning associated with that watermark. If you place your life on the line to enter the inorganic world, this is creating a watermark. Integrating it as part of a complete cohesion represents having learned that ability. To gain the stability of entering a new world, you need to be open and flexible, yet resolute.

For another example, say you're experimenting with a variety of diets to find out what works for you. Once you firmly decide on a course of action, you draw your line in the sand and agree not to backslide into prior habits. By enacting your decision, you've created a watermark. You were open and flexible so you could develop a new watermark, then by decisive action, you gained a stable reference to pursue more learning.

This procedure also helps you learn how to learn. By working through the watermark process, you become more adept at self-motivated learning.

Intelligence

Once upon a time, intelligence was directly related to a score, an intelligence quotient, commonly known as "IQ." In recent years, this has been challenged as being a very limited perspective of human capabilities. Some say IQ measurements are culturally biased, others say it focuses too much on intellectual capacities; still others say it's just plain obsolete.

In addition to the emotional intelligence Goleman writes about, research indicates that intelligence surfaces in many ways. For example, in his groundbreaking book *Frames of Mind: The Theory of Multiple Intelligences*, educator Howard Gardner provides evidence that humans have within themselves a number of different intelligences. He says "human beings have evolved to exhibit several intelligences and not to draw variously on one flexible intelligence."[1] In other words, we have more going for us than just the intellect. While the intellect may be flexible, pinning intelligence solely to its realm is not. Included among the various intelligences, Gardner says we have those of language, music, the physical body, and social adeptness. He even suggests that there is a *spiritual* intelligence.[2] From this perspective, each chakra energy contains its own intelligence, as do each of the cornerstones of perception. In turn, trackers and dreamers exhibit their own special variety of intelligence.

Intelligence may be defined as "the ability to meet and adapt to novel situations; the ability to utilize abstract concepts effectively; and the ability to grasp relationships and to learn quickly."[3] Gardner defines intelligence as the ability "to resolve genuine problems or difficulties."[4] He adds that "possession of an intelligence is most accurately thought of as a *potential* [italics his]."[5] Pure potential, then, is pure intelligence. It embodies all forms of intelligence, and it all waits to be tapped in a variety of ways.

In each instance, we have the ability to meet potential, to apply what is perceived, and to integrate the resulting experiences. This profile of intelligence may then be applied to whatever situation is at hand, be it working with mathematics, composing music, *seeing*, or dipping into the social structure of the inorganic world. Therefore, since evolving the energy body relies on meeting a greater potential of energy, awakening new cohesions, and applying the results, intelligence may also be thought of as the ability to manage cohesion. Accordingly, plugging into potential is intelligent. Bringing your predilections to life is intelligent. Evolving through your energy body is intelligent.

This brings us to what don Juan refers to as the *social base*.

The Social Base

A social base, according to don Juan, is a mold of thought, a template that governs how we think. One effect of our current template, for instance, is thinking that the world is made up of material objects, and, what is more important, having us behave as though this were entirely true. This material relationship with the world occurred after thousands of years of evolution, after thousands of years of knowledge being handed down generation to generation. The resulting perceptions from this legacy were then locked in place, thereby creating a huge self-fulfilling prophecy.

But, as you might imagine, this heritage is lacking. It is incomplete. For example, since the idea of the second energy field was never incorporated into their social base, don Juan says that white people (most likely referring to those who share a western-European materialistic philosophy) don't even know that it exists (*Tales*, 140). How true this is (or was) is a moot point in that it's a great lesson all by itself as it illustrates the dynamics of a social base. Thankfully, however, due in part to don Juan's teachings, we're now expanding our options to include new behaviors, including those derived from the second field.

Learning, then, is transformational. It's evolutionary. Typically, though, our options for transformation, to exercise intelligence, are limited by the social base, by what societies have agreed is proper. Thus, using physics to create a means to annihilate our planet is acceptable within the social base, levitating is not.

Don Juan also thinks that we are at a stage in our evolution where, if we are to survive, we must learn a new social base, and apply intelligence. A new social base for survival is one that prioritizes the world as energy. Material objects exist, he says, but only in relation to a world of energy (*Dreaming*, ch. 1).

To further illustrate, modern technology is an extension of our current social base. Manifesting technology relies on viewing the world as material, then projecting onto that world our thoughts about what we want created. We couldn't create computers, for example, unless the entire package existed within our awareness, within our potential. A social base also carries more subtle implications. For instance, we elevate the social standing of those who can perform tasks meaningful to the social base. Since physicists and physicians are skilled within a materialistic world, for example, they are given high status within ordinary society. In this same world, metaphysicists and healers tend to be looked at askance; that is, unless you're dealing with a metaphysical social base. Then metaphysicists and healers are seen as having substantial influence.

In each case, arbitrarily deciding who, or what, is intelligent sends the message that we should be self-important; otherwise, what's the point of elevating one's social standing? In each case, social status is arbitrary since this type of thinking stems from the social base. It is self-importance because it combines self-enhancement and self-reflection. That's a heck of a thing to transcend. It's a whole heaping helping of power, which restrains cohesion to the social base. What's more, within a social base, this power is amplified because we *feel* like we know what's going on, let alone just *thinking* that we know.

It is this collective of feeling that author Stuart Wilde refers to as "popular emotion."[6] Being popular is always of a social base, and therefore of one conditional field or another. As a result, these mental and emotional links among people produce projection on a mass scale. This projection is the social base.

To help us understand the social base better, don Juan refers to the topic of *uniformity*. From chapter two, remember that uniformity pertains to the shape of the energy body. In general terms, each generation shares a common uniformity. Thus, each generation perceives the world similarly. Since cohesion is a pattern of energy within the energy body, uniformity has a profound influence on it. Uniformity determines what kinds of energy patterns can exist within its boundaries. Hence, each generation also has a similar, overall cohesion.

The energy bodies of the old cycle of Toltecs, for example, had more of an oblong shape than exists today. Maybe this is why they lost themselves in bizarre, and often aberrant, practices. By contrast, the evolution of the human energy body is such that it's becoming more spherical (*Dreaming,* ch. 1). Therefore, the new uniformity is automatically producing changes in cohesion, which is automatically changing perception, which is automatically changing behavior. Perhaps this evolution is lending itself to a more balanced cohesion, and thus more balanced behavior. Perhaps this accounts for the modern spiritual renaissance that many people refer to as the *New Age*.

To track freedom, you must step beyond the social base. If you don't, you'll remain within the confines of a conditional field. One way to liberate your energy body is to recapitulate your life, including the nature of the times you live. Doing so separates your social self from your life force.[7] Having accomplished this, you stand a better chance of tapping pure potential, not just the potential within the social base. As a result, you awaken the complete intelligence of your energy body, not just one variety of it.

Let's not forget petty tyrants. Don Juan says that they are not only to help you lose self-importance, they are to help you perform the "very sophisticated maneuver" of stepping out of this world (*Fire,* 42). When you peak your relation to potential, you're automatically inaccessible to the energies of form. Any conditional energy field is of form, whether it be that of an individual, the social base, or complete fields of energy. A petty tyrant gives you training to peak potential by requiring that you intend your awareness away from the full force of conditional energy; after all, it's having an excessively regimented cohesion that turns a person into a petty tyrant. Plus, if you can't meet, then sidestep, the highly focused conditional energy of a petty tyrant, you stand a good chance of becoming one yourself. This is because your cohesion will entrain to, and then stabilize, that type of energy, that type of behavior. However, by working with this entire process of plugging into potential, you are delivered deeper into potential, and, therefore, closer to freedom.

According to Clara, one of Abelar's teachers, another tip to help you untether yourself from the social base is to develop *invisibility*, or calm indifference. Doing so helps you enter realms "where humanness doesn't count."[8] Invisibility, she says, is akin to gazing inwardly. It also relates to *seeing*, which, as previously mentioned, occurs when you become nothing by becoming everything.

Calm indifference also helps you track your core energy. Your core, remember, is of pure potential. It's not the socially defined energy that exists in the cohesion surrounding the core. You're aiming for the cool spot in the center of the flame. Getting there, and staying there, is what grooming a natural energy field is all about. It's a dance with pure potential. It's a way to become invisible while becoming your complete self.

Now, if you're out there merging with potential, you're in a wide-open ball game. There is no right or wrong in potential. Everything exists. Everything has its place. To handle this power, you need a sense of balance, not to mention a sense of humor. Otherwise, you'll think it's fine and dandy to harm your neighbors, even if it's just inflicting them with what you think is right. In the Toltec world, balance comes from the ethical considerations derived from traveling a path with heart.

The Evolution of Perception

I don't think it's too far-fetched to say that our current line of evolution is in line with ET technologies. Reason is evolving, and thereby becoming more capable of handling out-of-this-world concepts. But there will most likely be a great time-lag getting up to speed with ETs. It'll probably take some time for humans to build a flying saucer, for instance. Our very own UFO, which is the equivalent of a time machine, is probably years in the making. Scientific theories will have to be put forward and tested for the social base to incorporate this type of technology.

Toltecs, on the other hand, speed up the evolutionary process by dreaming, and then relying on tracking for direction and stability. Teleportation, for example, is having time-travel abilities without an external technology, like a UFO.

Toltec abilities are derived, says don Juan, from *silent knowledge*, from awareness that is within us but outside the domain of reason. Silent knowledge is a comprehensive knowing, a sense of natural order. Like other stable perceptions, it is a focal point position. Don Juan adds that years upon years ago, this was the natural condition of being human: that of behaving from silent knowledge. Then something occurred that created reason within us; from that point we entered an evolutionary track concerned with objectifying our environment. Therefore, the sense of being separate from the world created objectivity, and vice versa. This new relationship with the world magnified the perception of living in a material world (*Silence,* ch. 6).

My speculation is that the evolutionary formation of the neomammalian brain (also known as the neocortex) produced this new relationship with the world. This is the part of the brain where abstract thinking is centered, and its formation produced reason.

Many people are already familiar with the horizontal partitioning of the brain; namely, the right and left hemispheres. But there is also a three-level, vertical partitioning. In sweeping generalizations, it turns out that the base of the brain, the reptilian section, involves the automatic regulation of the physical body. Our heart beat and breathing, for instance, are maintained by this area. The midbrain, or paleomammalian section, has within it the limbic system, which regulates emotions. The neomammalian section deals with abstract reasoning.[9] Thus we have a variety of hardware within the brain, along with the functions of intelligence that each provides.

You don't have to have the whole mix to be intelligent, though. This kind of thinking is obsolete, not to mention self-important. Casual observation demonstrates that other mammals without a neocortex behave in an intelligent manner. Wolves, for example, are social creatures, have their own rules, and can hunt with the best. They act through some form of instinct, from some form of silent knowledge. Humans seem to be unique in that they regard themselves as separate from the environment. This has estranged us from our very life source, and may well be producing the effects don Juan warns about.

Fortunately, we can take the perceptions objectivity provides, and apply them toward enhancing our evolution. It's objectivity that allows us to understand understanding; pure understanding is knowing that the world is a mystery. In addition, even though don Juan thinks technology makes us sterile, he also says Toltecs choose both options of living in a material world, and of living in a world of energy (*Dreaming*, 4). So, perhaps technology will help turn the tide in favor of helping all humans learn freedom.

In a fuller sense, technology includes the structures of metaphysical philosophies—nontraditional technologies, if you will. Indeed, using a biblical allegory, don Juan says that being cast out from the Garden of Eden is a way of saying that we lost our silent knowledge. The Toltec Way, he says, is a path leading back to that paradise (*Silence*, 122–123). This doesn't mean we have to forget everything we've learned. We can use reason and understanding to help us recapture silent knowledge.

Maybe we must command reason to again track silent knowledge. If so, this is what having a well-built launch pad provides. Steps leading up to the launch pad include giving yourself new options of behavior, stopping your internal dialogue, stopping the world, and beefing up body knowledge. Hence, you have the power of a logically created philosophy generating power to enhance your evolution into, and through, silent knowledge.

In fact, to make this process work even better, we can use our objective, rational sense. Drawing on the work of psychologist Charles Tart, for example, let's examine the process of perceptual evolution. In his book, *States of Consciousness*, Tart puts forth the concepts of *baseline state of consciousness* (b-SoC), *altered state of consciousness* (ASoC), and *discrete altered state of consciousness* (d-ASoC).[10] In a nutshell, a b-SoC is your normal, waking consciousness, your normal cohesion. An ASoC is a state of consciousness that in some way differs from a b-SoC; thus, an altered state. A d-ASoC is a stable, usable altered state. A discrete state may be returned to time and again. Thus, spontaneously levitating is an altered state; knowing how to do it on command results from having a discrete altered state, from being able to produce, at *will*, a "levitation" cohesion.

Let's relate this dynamic to evolving your energy body through a number of cohesions. To do so, start with a stable cohesion. It doesn't matter what kind it is, ordinary or nonordinary. To change an entire baseline state, you need to experience a number of different cohesions. This is where experience with the gait of power, elemental spirits, the inorganic world, and dreaming pays off, for example.

Now then, to get from one cohesion to another, as well as from one baseline to another, you first need to suspend your current cohesion. This is where gazing, nonpatterning, and stopping the internal dialogue all come in handy. Then you need to destabilize your cohesion. You need to get it loose and free, ready to accept new experiences. Again, nonpatterning helps. Next, add erasing personal history, altering routines, and stopping the world, and you come up with a special mix that lets you slide away. Literally. But since you don't want to slide any which way, you need intent.

Intent is what shifts cohesion. In this case, having a purpose for why you want to shift your cohesion is part of your intent. Your purpose keeps you on track toward evolving your cohesion, not just experiencing random nonsense. To re-stabilize your cohesion, which is the next step, you definitely need purpose. Throw in some very solid and meaningful predilection shields, and you're back up and running. You've stabilized a new cohesion, or baseline, depending on what you're working on.

Having a number of altered states can give you sufficient experience to help you stabilize a new cohesion. Several spontaneous OBEs, for instance, may give you such a sense of the ability that you can produce the "OBE" cohesion at *will*. As a result, OBEs will have become a discrete altered state. In like manner, if you have a number of different discrete states, you can change your entire baseline state. That is, if you have solid, discrete experiences concerning reincarnation, out-of-body experiences, talks with elemental spirits, channeling, and other metaphysical experiences, you change your entire cohesion. Thus, you've changed your baseline state, which means you've changed the world you live in.

The social base is a baseline state on a mass scale. Therefore, what occurs on a metaphysical path is an altered state in relation to an ordinary baseline. An OBE would be considered an altered state for most participants within an ordinary reality, for instance. In turn, since practitioners of metaphysics can bring forth different altered states, they have formed a discrete altered state in relation to the ordinary baseline. They may summon different-than-ordinary perceptions. If a practitioner is very skilled, then a new baseline—a nonordinary baseline—has been formed. Put a bunch of these people in a room, and you have a new social base.

Taking this one more step, for most metaphysical practitioners, the baseline of a person of knowledge is an altered state. It is that dramatic a shift from the cohesions of systems, even when they have been fully integrated.

By knowing how this process works, you can build a foundation to support it. You can then take deliberate steps to bring your evolution about. In terms of the Toltec Way, you have used reason to create channel markers to help you evolve beyond reason and into *will*. By doing so, you transcend the limitations of the intellect, and regain the wondrous capacities of the entire body.

Just keep in mind that changing your b-SoC a time or two doesn't mean you've found freedom. It may mean you've just found more entertainment. By changing your social base from an ordinary world to a nonordinary world, you've gained knowledge of the process, and what the changes represent. Then you need to reapply all that you've learned to evolve your nonordinary baseline into yet another new baseline. In other words, after you've stabilized a nonordinary baseline, you must still put in the work to experience new altered states, and then discrete altered states, so that you may continue to evolve into the baseline of a natural energy field.

A Learning Posture

Just like it's possible to examine the workings of reason, then apply what's learned to evolve beyond reason, it's possible to examine learning, then apply those studies to quicken the process. All tracking and dreaming exercises, for example, serve to facilitate learning. Indeed, the Toltec system, itself, is a way to learn how to learn. Each of your watermarks, for instance, represents something learned. Each shift in cohesion also represents learning, as does working through altered states to a new baseline. So watch out! Learning is happening all over the place. Forging a path with heart is one way to make sure that what you learn is purposeful.

Many basic skills that promote learning are presented in chapter four. Each of those behaviors in some way adds to your skill of managing your energy body. This, in turn, automatically opens the way for you to remember what is within and without; when you tune in to your nature, learning becomes natural.

To help you do it just a little bit better, here are five tips—five behaviors—that promote learning. Just like all the other exercises, keep working with them to elevate your level of skill.

Maintain cool effort. Don't bash you head into walls. Don't try to force the world into compliance with your wishes. Learn what the world *is*. In addition, don't work by another person's timetable. Have a little fun finding out the natural rhythms of your life. Then relax, be patient, and let your energy body breathe.

Exercise a high level of inquiry. Stay open and flexible. Keep asking questions. Don't settle for an answer when your body yearns for more. Plus, look at the evidence, look at what occurred, at what is. Use all of your experience: past, present, and future (if you can stretch into it), and let your prior experiences be rendered obsolete if necessary. As the philosopher Arthur Schopenhauer says. "the contemplation and observation of everything *actual*, as soon as it presents something new to the observer, is more instructive than all reading and hearing about it."[11]

Acknowledge complete responsibility. For all your behavior, for all that you perceive, and for everything that results from your inquiries.

Sustain the pursuit of objectivity. Now, really folks, if there is an illusion, it's this thing called "objectivity." By applying the lessons of the focal point, we know that anything we perceive is simultaneously real and illusory. Therefore, objectivity is objective only in relation to what is under scrutiny. At the same time, objectivity is the saving grace of all your efforts. It's what keeps you from lying to yourself, and to others. It's what allows you to accurately observe yourself, others, and the world. In short, objectivity is ruthlessness.

Remember the Alamo. As brave as you are, death is waiting to nail you. All your fine learning is waiting to be rendered null and void. You'll either find your awareness in a new dimension, with a grander scale of learning to be tackled, or your awareness will be extinguished. In the first case, you've left your current known world and the unknown beckons, which means you once again get to let go of what you now hold as true in order to claim new knowledge. In the second instance, it doesn't much matter. You're history. Learning doesn't even enter the picture if you're not aware of anything.

Let's assume you get to continue learning, and you retain what you've learned. Toltec-like training can continue helping you, even if you find yourself in a completely new dimension, requiring a brand-new orientation. For example, when you're working with pure understanding, you're dealing directly with mystery. You have a complete sense that something more awaits, a sense of discovery, always. In broad strokes, if you take the ordinary conditional thinking that we live only in a material world, then overlay that energy with a bit of nonordinary conditional thinking that includes such things as multiple realities, teleportation, and ability to step in and out of dimensions, you have quite a powerhouse of thought on your hands. At the same time, if both of these worlds are forms of conditional energy, then what's next? What magnificence lies ahead, naturally?

15

STRAIGHT
FROM
THE
HEART

There's a wicked spell floating around. It goes like this: "If I know the thoughts, I know." The longer version is "If can talk fluently about past lives, psychic phenomena, near-death experiences, out-of-body experiences, elemental spirits, and other metaphysical topics, then, of course, I know."

Wow, just when you thought you had enough of my talk about not getting hung up in a system, here's a whole chapter on it. This is something don Juan drilled into me, and I guess the karma of it is that you're getting the same. The idea is this: When you're able to talk the lingo of a system, and things start making sense, it's all very seductive. All this tracking and dreaming, for instance, is very easy to get lost in because it's all so very cool. To head trouble off at the pass, let's look at some ins and outs of fundamentalism, then be on our way.

Any cohesive, alternative lifestyle carries great power, enough power to have its adherents bolt away from conventional society, or at least regard themselves as somehow removed from the ordinary flow of society. Whether it be a cult, a corporation, an intentional community centered around shared values, or a metaphysical path, the adherents of any alternative social grouping develop some version of a nonordinary conditional energy field. Participants of mainstream society also develop a conditional field, the ordinary one we've chatted about. In general, then, a gathering of like-minded people generates power; sometimes for better, sometimes for worse.

The better of it is that a group can usually accumulate knowledge faster than one person alone. The more personalities and predilections you have out there exploring the unknown, the greater the results. The worse of it is that the social base that comes from these explorations may be misconstrued as being true reality. Whether this distortion comes from scientists, religious leaders, or philosophers, it is *fundamentalism*. Indeed, anytime you try to define, confine, or otherwise limit awareness—anytime you step away from pure potential—you have fundamentalism. We have to knock it off to get on with the program of tracking freedom.

Fundamentalism may occur at any stage of growth. Whether you're an apprentice or a Toltec, your principal energy is conditional. It isn't until you break into the person of knowledge stage that you've reduced the influence of this type of energy. Even if you've groomed a natural energy field, losing yourself in your personal relationship with the world is still something to watch out for.

For many years, we've been in the midst of the New Age movement, a great renaissance of thought and experience. The main thrust of it centers on awakening spirituality. New Agers explore past lives, meditation, alternative healing, new relationships with God, just to name a few items on the agenda. Yet, much of this "new" agenda has already been very well established in philosophies around the world. Perhaps what makes it "new" is the amount of attention given to it, and the number of people taking up its reins. If this is true, the New Age movement could be considered a result of changes in the human energy body's uniformity and cohesion. As mentioned in the previous chapter, the human energy body is evolving into a more spherical shape. Its uniformity is changing. If so, this would lend itself to more people perceiving a more holistic world, which is very much part of the New Age.

Like specific metaphysical philosophies, New Age thought in general is far-reaching, and often touches every aspect of a person's life. Indeed, since it could be considered an umbrella for all metaphysical philosophies, it carries immense power. However, just like the ground we covered when addressing a single philosophy, New Age thought is just another social base.

As a structure of thinking about reality, the social base relies on many people achieving a consensus worldview. But don Juan says that the social base loses its power when we realize we're working with an inherited set of outdated assumptions about reality, rather than establishing an ongoing re-examination of our lot as humans (*Dreaming,* 4).

When you're outside the social base, and you're continuing to learn in leaps and bounds, you're truly connected with guidance from Spirit. That is, Spirit is giving you a way to proceed. Again, though, here's the trap. By knowing you're working with Spirit guidance, and this is what New Agers do, you think you're really getting on with the program. Plus, you'll have lots of people agreeing with you that you're now engaging the world the way it really is. You'll then rejoice in finding membership within your new social base. Freedom, however, is found completely beyond the social base, and completely within the bosom of Spirit, not within any template of thinking, be it ordinary or metaphysical.

Thus, while New Age thinking gives you direction, and gives you ways to proceed, it is of finite form and is therefore not the pure art of infinite potential. To fully grasp this, you must be willing to leave all social ties, and stand alone while looking into the heart of creation. Then go back and cultivate your social connections. Indeed, for most, they are part of a path with heart. Just be careful, as your clarity may have you thinking you've got it all down straight when you really don't.

Examples of Fundamentalism

To avoid the pitfalls of fundamentalism, it's necessary to accept the legitimacy of other points of view, especially if they conflict with your own views. The universe is a wide-open place. Why confine it to your pet thoughts? If we let go and constantly challenge our assumptions, our pet thoughts will change, or even become obsolete. Within the New Age movement, and within traditional metaphysical philosophies, there are a variety of slogans, tips to get you on the path. Let's poke among these for a bit. Challenge them at *will*.

God said it, I believe it, that settles it. Great bumper sticker. It provides thrust for stepping outside the social base, and connecting with a higher—if not the highest—power. But how do you know God really said it? And are you going to take your guidance and inflict it on others?

It's an illusion. Yeah, it's an illusion in relation to other points of view. But using the model of cohesion and the focal point, we could also say that everything is real. It's just a matter of formulating a cohesion, just a matter of stabilizing a focal point. That's what makes something real. In relation to this, everything else is an illusion. Indeed, any focal point position is an illusion when you compare it with infinite potential. Yet that thought stems from a focal point position, and this makes it real in its own way.

There are no mistakes. This perspective definitely opens you up to infinite potential, knowing that there is perfection in each and every event that occurs throughout creation, but give me a break. You never screwed up? This doesn't mean you can't learn from your mistakes, and thereby make something good out of them. But you give your power away by the bucket when you think you'll never make a mistake.

I'm anchoring the energies. Whew! Self-importance in action here, folks. Once upon a time, a good friend of mine had a girlfriend. After a hot-and-heavy, two-month affair, she dumped him, which is fair enough. As a reason for the breakup, she said that her job to bring in and anchor energies from a more spiritual dimension was finished, and now she was off to another town to do the same. So bye-bye. He deserved it, getting tangled up with her like he did, but I really think she was the one who needed an anchor. Projection, anyone?

I smoke to ground myself. I've heard this one more than once. Personally speaking, I drink soda pop to bring myself back from dreaming. The bubbles stimulate my physical body. We're both nuts. The remedy is to find some better shields—some deeper predilections—to restore our balance, and to ground us.

You create your own reality. After all, this is what manifesting from personal responsibility is all about. But maybe this slogan really doesn't hold all that much power. After all, it is a philosophical assumption. It is not fact, even though we can see it working in our lives.

A slogan only holds power if you use it consistently, and take it all the way, not just for how long it's convenient. In other words, you have to assume responsibility for everything in your life, including your neighbors and how they affect you. This doesn't mean you are responsible for your neighbors; it means you're responsible for having those neighbors in your life. In this manner, you unveil deeper levels of yourself. By going deeper and deeper, you come to your core, you get to a point where you would no longer interpret or define the world, in such a way as "you create your own reality." By then you've grown out of the system, the philosophy and structures that once applied pressure to make you grow.

Maybe the pressure from the Eagle's emanations on our energy bodies generates our decisions. In other words, maybe a decision occurs by acquiescing to a cohesion, be it dysfunctional or positive. Because we've learned to develop reason and objectivity, we conjure up the perception that somehow we are the ones really making the decisions.

Earth is a school. There's no doubt that learning takes place in humans. Exactly what is learned may be open to question, but, for good or ill, humans learn. In general, what is learned is more and more about the human condition. By doing so, we remember what's already in store, or better yet, what's in the energy body. Therefore, saying "Earth is a school" is a projection of the natural tendency to learn, thereby making the environment a place of learning. Again, learning is also a remembrance. But what the heck life *is*, what it *really* is, and what it really is *for*, is a mystery. To regard it otherwise locks the door to potential. (How's that for some sophisticated fundamentalist thinking?)

It was supposed to happen. Says who?

There's a reason for everything. Sure, you can find a reason for anything, but that doesn't mean that there is a reason for it. To have "a reason for it" requires relating the experience to a specific logic, or to a complete worldview. In so doing, you equate the particular logic with the reason at hand. Do this enough and you have a conditional energy field, be it ordinary or nonordinary. The difference being that an ordinary field would have a reason such as "you are adept at mathematics because you have genetic makeup that lends itself to math." A nonordinary reason would be "you are adept at mathematics because you have good karma from a past life."

Now, a metaphysicist would also say "you have a genetic makeup that lends itself to math because you have good karma from a past life." This enhanced accountability is what makes fundamentalism such a hard rap to beat. Since you can account for more, you get to thinking that you have the inside scoop.

We live in a world of duality. Yes, we do. This is because we have a two-sided horizontal brain: the right and left hemispheres. This hardwiring has us again projecting innate tendencies onto the external world. The world becomes dualistic because of the way information is regulated and processed by the brain.

By looking at the brain's structure, we can also see why Toltecs say there are three energy fields. Remember that in addition to right and left partitioning, there is a three-level, vertical partitioning relating to physical, emotional, and abstract-mental functions, with the vertical segments corresponding to the first, second, and third fields, respectively.

Creating this world of energy fields is definitely projecting and molding the body into the structure of a philosophy. However, it seems very workable in that this philosophy is nature based. By relating your worldview directly to the natural condition, you stand a better chance of figuring out what the human condition is.

Well, there you have it. A few examples of what people say that keeps them focused in fundamentalism. Don't forget to challenge everything; right, *everything.*

Staying on the Tuna Boat

There's no doubt that the fundamentals of a system serve to liberate perception. They keep you sailing toward your destination, and make the journey the essence of your life. It's only when you lose yourself in the fundamentals that you fall overboard.

So here are some tips and reminders on how to free perception.

1. Don't use your knowledge as an excuse not to look at yourself.
2. Learn to *see*, as doing so suspends conditional fields.
3. Shift your focal point. Fundamentalists try to maintain a certain perspective, which means maintaining a particular focal point position.
4. Cultivate a bent for examination, for understanding. Don Juan calls this *sobriety*, which automatically leads to a shift in the focal point (*Fire,* 178).
5. Challenge all the assumptions that make up your worldview.
6. Don't let your love for the fundamentals turn you into a fundamentalist.
7. Don't confuse intellectual fluency with having the ability of what it is you're talking about.
8. Just because you have an experience—like a NDE—doesn't mean you know, either. Remember that there are different interpretations of what it means to visit the white light.
9. Get comfortable with not knowing anything.

Most of these perspectives are from a Toltec social base. Some may be found in some very hot books that are sweeping mainstream audiences, such as in the international bestsellers *The Celestine Prophecy*, by James Redfield, and the

Conversations with God books by Neale Donald Walsch.[1] As a result, millions of people are being exposed to, and influenced by, this type of thinking, be they New Agers or not. When you have so many people forming a new pattern of thought, you have a revolution on your hands.

Yet, for the revolutionary transformation of freedom, even this power must be transcended. Supplanting one template of thought for another does not make a recipe for complete evolution. You need to add the ingredients of self-empowerment, personal responsibility, independent thinking and feeling, nonattachment, fluidity, constantly challenging assumptions about reality, losing self-importance (*especially* losing self-importance), and everything else that a workable philosophy provides—including leaving the philosophy behind. Do you *see* the situation?

The bottom line is that fundamentalists turn the work of evolution into acts of self-importance. As members of the flock, fundamentalists find meaning within social understandings. On the other hand, a person of knowledge finds meaning by matching personal energies with pure potential, then letting life unfold from there. From this relationship, each and every step of life is a renewal, not a repetition of form. As you can sense, being a fundamentalist isn't as much fun as tracking freedom.

Evaluating a Philosophy

Part of the work of letting pet slogans become obsolete is developing a new set of perspectives, preferably one that enhances evolution. There's a lot of tracking that must be done for this, and it comes under the heading of reconnaissance. For successful recon missions, you must remain relaxed and balanced. You must know what pieces of your thinking fit where, and why. As such, part of the work of tracking freedom is remaining true to a philosophy while remaining true to yourself. Unless you're somehow gifted, you need a system for its enlarged worldview, its channel markers to keep you on track, and its how-to-do-it skills to bring about your evolution. These markers may be simple tips. For example, don Juan advised Castaneda not to become overconfident. Toltec practices, he says, can be deadly and there's no time to be fooling around (*Dreaming,* 104).

This is backed up with traditional scientific research. Arthur Deikman, M.D., for example, in his landmark study of cult behavior, *The Wrong Way Home,* found that overconfidence leads to the demise of spiritual organizations, if not individual people.[2]

Needless to say, you won't get very far if you get lost, or even drown, in the channel, which means you've lost the sense of tracking your core energies. In this light, a viable philosophy always has two features that indicate whether it's strong enough, and flexible enough, to get you to your core. We touched on this in chapter one, but it bears repeating.

The first indicator of a viable system is that it's nonexclusive. It won't shunt ideas, practices, procedures, worldviews, and goals away from anyone. It opens doors for all. Now, whether its practitioners actually follow the path they preach about is another story. That's a fight with self-importance. For instance, Deikman found that self-righteousness is a marked feature of cult members.[3] Embarking on a path of self-importance is contrary to staying on the boat. It only leads into room after room of mirror images of yourself, or rather of the images you have of yourself. That won't get you too far. Therefore, perhaps the attitude that there are only a few chosen Toltecs floating around out there is also an indication of cult behavior. Indeed, Deikman found that devaluing outsiders was a firm indication of cult activity.[4]

The second indicator of a viable system is that the philosophy clearly teaches that it is only a means to an end. It is to help generate clarity, not lock perception in its clarity. Author John Van Auken has observed that phenomena, or elements within a worldview, can blind you to the greater glory of Spirit, or they can serve as a bridge to it.[5] The idea being that having fun with elemental spirits, omens, psychic phenomena, and the like can open the way to a greater sense and vision of the world. Or, your experiences will have you thinking that they are the world, and you'll be so enthralled that you'll forget about the work of hooking up with Spirit. If you're not sailing the high seas of the unknown for that destination, then you've fallen off the tuna boat!

Now, if you happen to think that the tuna boat is a smelly proposition (which it certainly is), let's check your balance. Are you saying so because you're concerned with ruthless accuracy? Or because you know it's just not your path? Or because you're devaluing others? Good questions to ask yourself anytime you scorn someone. Always keep in mind that fishermen work very hard to deliver food to your table. Please feel free to expand this analogy to other areas of your life. Anyway, back to sailing the high seas.

Having wide-ranging effects, developing a path with heart is a comprehensive way to give yourself room to explore the oceans of the universe while remaining true to your primary goal. In a manner of speaking, it helps you learn to walk on water so that when you fall off the boat you can climb back on board.

In addition, other features of the Toltec system—such as tracking the stages of evolution, and developing the levels of dreaming—might help you literally walk on water, as doing so is a form of levitation. By then you're ready to be on your own. You've gone from an ordinary to a nonordinary conditional energy field, and are ready to form a natural field. Since you've been tracking freedom for a while now, take a little time to remember what it took to manifest your goals. Recapitulate the journey of evolving your energy body. Then, by claiming your knowledge, you're well prepared to fly away from the boat, soar away from the water, and head off toward freedom.

So, for personal, radical evolution remain true to yourself, and live your life straight from the heart.

NOTES

Chapter 1. What's Up?

1. References from the works of Carlos Castaneda are cited in the text using the following abbreviations:

Teachings:
> *The Teachings of Don Juan: A Yaqui Way of Knowledge* (New York: Simon & Schuster, 1968).

Separate:
> *A Separate Reality: Further Conversations with Don Juan* (New York: Simon & Schuster, 1971).

Journey:
> *Journey to Ixtlan: The Lessons of Don Juan* (New York: Simon & Schuster, 1972).

Tales:
> *Tales of Power* (New York: Simon & Schuster, 1974).

Second Ring:
> *The Second Ring of Power* (New York: Simon & Schuster, 1977).

Gift:
> *The Eagle's Gift* (New York: Simon & Schuster, 1981).

Fire:
> *The Fire from Within* (New York: Simon & Schuster, 1984).

Silence:
> *The Power of Silence: Further Lessons of Don Juan* (New York: Simon & Schuster, 1987).

Dreaming:
> *The Art of Dreaming* (New York: HarperCollins, 1993).

2. The Monroe Institute, 62 Robert Mountains Road, Faber, VA 22938, (804) 361-1252.
3. The term "stalking" is used throughout Castaneda's books. I use the term "tracking," as I think it better represents the energy embodied within the skill.

Chapter 2. The World as Energy

1. Michael and Michele Flamingo, *Surfing Spirit: A Toltec Trip to the Beach* (as yet unpublished).
2. Brenda I. Koerner, "Is There Life After Death," *U.S. News & World Report*, March 31, 1997.

Chapter 3. Your Energy Resources

1. Diagram adapted with permission from *Das Wissen der Tolteken* (*The Knowledge of the Toltecs*), by Norbert Classen. (Eurasburg, Germany: edition tonal, 1992).
2. Taisha Abelar, *The Sorcerers' Crossing: A Woman's Journey* (New York: Viking, 1992), p. xii.
3. Daniel Goleman, "Anatomy of an Emotional Hijacking," chap. 2 in *Emotional Intelligence* (New York: Bantam Books, 1995).
4. Goleman, p. 43.

Chapter 4. Entering the Void

1. Goleman, p. 65.
2. J.P. Chaplin, *Dictionary of Psychology* (New York: Dell Publishing, 1975), p. 411.
3. Works cited include
   a. Castaneda, *Journey to Ixtlan*.
   b. Victor Sanchez, *The Teachings of Don Carlos,* trans. Robert Nelson (Santa Fe, N.M.: Bear & Co., 1995).

   c. Ken Eagle Feather, *Traveling With Power* and
       A Toltec Path (Charlottesville, Virginia: Hamp-
       ton Roads Publishing Co., 1992 and 1995).
4. Shunryu Suzuki, *Zen Mind, Beginner's Mind* (New
   York: Weatherhill, 1970), p. 119.

Chapter 5. Stability Stabilizes

1. Barbara Tedlock, "The Clown's Way," chap. 7 in
   Teachings from the American Earth, Dennis and
   Barbara Tedlock, eds. (New York: Liveright, 1975).
2. Works cited include
   a. Castaneda, *The Art of Dreaming*.
   b. Abelar, *The Sorcerers' Crossing*.
   c. Sanchez, *The Teachings of Don Carlos*.
   d. Feather, *A Toltec Path*.
3. Abelar, pp. 50–57.
4. Goleman, pp. 62–65.
5. A. M. Gray, *Warfighting: The U.S. Marine Corps Book
   of Strategy* (New York: Doubleday, 1989), p. 13.
6. Goleman, pp. 86–88.

Chapter 6. Spellbound

1. Gal. 6:7 King James Bible.

Chapter 7. Manifestly Yours

1. PSI Research, "Visualization Improves Athletic
   Success," *Venture Inward* 11, no. 4 (July/August
   1995).
2. Marsha Sinetar, *Do What You Love, the Money
   Will Follow: Discovering Your Right Livelihood*
   (Mahwah, N.J.: Paulist Press, 1987).
3. Huston Smith, *The World's Religions: Our Great
   Wisdom Traditions* (New York: HarperCollins,
   1991).

Chapter 8. It Helps to Have a Cement Truck

1. Abelar, p. 231.
2. Florinda Donner, *Being-in-Dreaming: An Initiation into the Sorcerers' World* (New York: Harper-Collins, 1991), p. 219.

Chapter 9. Launch Pad 101

1. Goleman, p. 36.
2. Courses at the Religious Studies Department, University of South Florida, Tampa, Fla.

Chapter 10. "Let's Get Physical" Is Just an Expression

1. Abelar, p. 102.
2. Frank Koelsch, *The Infomedia Revolution* (Toronto: McGraw-Hill Ryerson, 1995), p. 129.
3. Keith Thompson, "Portrait of a Sorcerer," *New Age Journal*, April 1994.
4. Francis Jeffrey and John Lilly, M.D., *John Lilly, So Far* (Los Angeles: Jeremy P. Tarcher, 1990).
5. Steve Aukstakalnis and David Blatner, *Silicon Mirage: The Art and Science of Virtual Reality* (Berkeley, Calif.: Peachpit Press, 1992), p. 21.
6. Aukstakalnis and Blatner, p. 22.
7. Glen O. Gabbard and Stuart Twemlow, *With the Eyes of the Mind* (New York: Praeger, 1984).
8. James Gleick, "The Butterfly Effect," chap. 1 in *Chaos: Making a New Science* (New York: Penguin Books, 1987).

Chapter 11. In Your Dreams

1. Thompson, *New Age Journal*.

Chapter 12. Living in Infinite Potential

1. Mihaly Csikszentmihalyi, *Flow: The Psychology of Optimal Experience* (New York: HarperPerennial, 1990), p. xi.
2. Goleman, p. 90.
3. Csikszentmihalyi, p. 26.
4. Csikszentmihalyi, p. 27.
5. Victor Sanchez, *Toltecs of the New Millennium,* trans. Robert Nelson (Santa Fe, N.M.: Bear & Co., 1996).
6. Kathy Sawyer, "Global Shift May Have Sped Evolution," *The Washington Post*, July 25, 1997.

Chapter 13. Guidance Systems

1. Csikszentmihalyi, p. 54.
2. Goleman, p. 62.
3. Goleman, p. 21.
4. Goleman, p. 293.
5. Julian Jaynes, *The Origin of Consciousness in the Breakdown of the Bicameral Mind* (Boston: Houghton Mifflin, 1977), pp. 236–246.

Chapter 14. It's Only Natural

1. Howard Gardner, *Frames of Mind: The Theory of Multiple Intelligences* (New York: HarperCollins, 1983), p. xii.
2. Gardner, p. xviii.
3. Chaplin, p. 263.
4. Gardner, p. 60.
5. Gardner, p. 68.
6. Stuart Wilde, *Infinite Self: 33 Steps to Reclaiming Your Inner Power* (Niles, Ill.: Nightingale-Conant, 1995).
7. Bruce Wagner, "You Only Live Twice," *Details*, March 1994, p. 214.

8. Abelar, pp. 66–67.

9. Richard M. Restak, M.D., "Answers to Questions Which Have Not Yet Been Raised," chap. 4 in *The Brain: The Last Frontier* (New York: Warner Books, 1979).

10. Charles T. Tart, *States of Consciousness* (New York: E. P. Dutton, 1975).

11. Arthur Schopenhauer, *The World as Will and Representation,* vol. 2, trans. E.F.J. Payne (New York: Dover Publications, Inc., 1969), p. 72.

Chapter 15. Straight from the Heart

1. Works cited include
   a. James Redfield, *The Celestine Prophecy* (New York: Warner Books, 1993).
   b. Neale Donald Walsch, *Conversations with God: an uncommon dialogue, Book 1* (New York: G. P. Putnam's Sons, 1996).
   c. Neale Donald Walsch, *Conversations with God: an uncommon dialogue, Book 2* (Charlottesville, Va.: Hampton Roads Publishing Co., 1997).

2. Arthur J. Deikman, M.D., *The Wrong Way Home: Uncovering the Patterns of Cult Behavior in American Society* (Boston: Beacon Press, 1990), p. 96.

3. Diekman, p. 105.

4. Deikman, p. 101.

5. John Van Auken, "Guides, Angels, and the Holy One," *Venture Inward* 10, no. 6 (July/August 1994).

Books Referenced

Abelar, Taisha. *The Sorcerers' Crossing: A Woman's Journey*. New York: Viking, 1992.

Aukstakalnis, Steve, and David Blatner. *Silicon Mirage: The Art & Science of Virtual Reality*. Berkeley, Calif.: Peachpit Press, 1992.

Castaneda, Carlos. *The Art of Dreaming*. New York: HarperCollins, 1993.

——. *The Eagle's Gift*. New York: Simon & Schuster, 1981.

——. *The Fire from Within*. New York: Simon & Schuster, 1984.

——. *Journey to Ixtlan: The Lessons of Don Juan*. New York: Simon & Schuster, 1972.

——. *The Power of Silence: Further Lessons of Don Juan*. New York: Simon & Schuster, 1987.

——. *The Second Ring of Power*. New York: Simon & Schuster, 1977.

——. *A Separate Reality: Further Conversations with Don Juan*. New York: Simon & Schuster, 1971.

——. *Tales of Power*. New York: Simon & Schuster, 1974.

——. *The Teachings of Don Juan: A Yaqui Way of Knowledge*. New York: Simon & Schuster, 1968.

Chaplin, J.P. *Dictionary of Psychology*. New York: Dell Publishing, 1975.

Classen, Norbert. *Das Wissen der Tolteken* (*The Knowledge of the Toltecs*). Eurasburg, Germany: edition tonal, 1992.

Csikszentmihalyi, Mihaly. *Flow: The Psychology of Optimal Experience*. New York: HarperPerennial, 1990.

Deikman, Arthur J., M.D. *The Wrong Way Home: Uncovering the Patterns of Cult Behavior in America*. Boston: Beacon Press, 1990.

Donner, Florinda. *Being-in-Dreaming: An Initiation into the Sorcerers' World*. New York: HarperCollins, 1991.

Feather, Ken Eagle. *Traveling With Power: The Exploration and Development of Perception*. Charlottesville, Va.: Hampton Roads Publishing Co., 1992.

———. *A Toltec Path: A User's Guide to the Teachings of don Juan Matus, Carlos Castaneda, and Other Toltec Seers*. Charlottesville, Va.: Hampton Roads Publishing Co., 1995.

Gabbard, Glen O., and Stuart Twemlow. *With the Eyes of the Mind: An Empirical Analysis of Out of Body States*. New York: Praeger, 1984.

Gardner, Howard. *Frames of Mind: The Theory of Multiple Intelligences*. New York: HarperCollins, 1983.

Gleick, James. *Chaos: Making a New Science*. New York: Penguin Books, 1987.

Goleman, Daniel. *Emotional Intelligence*. New York: Bantam Books, 1995.

y, A. M., *Warfighting: The U.S. Marine Corps Book of Strategy*. ew York: Doubleday, 1989.

ulian. *The Origin of Consciousness in the Breakdown of meral Mind*. Boston: Houghton Mifflin, 1977.

is, and John Lilly, M.D. *John Lilly, So Far*. Los emy P. Tarcher, 1990.

Koelsch, Frank. *The Infomedia Revolution: How It Is Changing Our World and Your Life*. Toronto: McGraw-Hill Ryerson, 1995.

Redfield, James. *The Celestine Prophecy*. New York: Warner Books, 1993.

Restak, Richard M., M.D. *The Brain: The Last Frontier*. New York: Warner Books, 1979.

Sanchez, Victor. *The Teachings of Don Carlos: Practical Applications of the Works of Carlos Castaneda,* translated by Robert Nelson. Santa Fe, N.M.: Bear & Co., 1995.

——. *Toltecs of the New Millennium,* translated by Robert Nelson. Santa Fe, N.M.: Bear & Co., 1996.

Schopenhauer, Arthur. *The World as Will and Representation,* vol. 2. Translated by E.F.J. Payne. New York: Dover Publications, Inc., 1969.

Sinetar, Marsha. *Do What You Love, the Money Will Follow: Discovering Your Right Livelihood*. Mahwah, N.J.: Paulist Press, 1987.

Smith, Huston. *The World's Religions: Our Great Wisdom Traditions*. New York: HarperCollins, 1991.

Suzuki, Shunryu. *Zen Mind, Beginner's Mind*. New York: Weatherhill, 1970.

Tart, Charles T. *States of Consciousness*. New York: E.P. Dutton, 1985.

Tedlock, Barbara. "The Clown's Way." In *Teachings From the American Earth: Indian Religion and Philosophy*, edited by Dennis and Barbara Tedlock. New York: Liveright, 1975.

Walsch, Neale Donald. *Conversations with God: an uncommon dialogue, Book 1*. New York: G. P. Putnam's Sons, 1996.

———. *Conversations with God: an uncommon dialogue, Book 2.* Charlottesville, Va.: Hampton Roads Publishing Co., 1997.

Wilde, Stuart. *Infinite Self: 33 Steps to Reclaiming Your Inner Power.* Niles, Ill.: Nightingale-Conant, 1995.

INDEX

Chapter subheadings and diagrams

Diagrams

ABOUT THE AUTHOR

Tracking Freedom is Ken Eagle Feather's third book exploring the nature of perception as it relates to the Toltec teachings of don Juan Matus. His first book, *Traveling with Power,* introduces Toltec teachings and describes how Ken met don Juan. His second book, *A Toltec Path*, provides greater insight into Toltec philosophy.

In addition to a ten-year apprenticeship with don Juan, Ken has served on the staff of the Association for Research and Enlightenment, part of the Edgar Cayce legacy, and has served on the staff of The Monroe Institute, founded by researcher Robert Monroe.

Hampton Roads Publishing Company

...for the evolving human spirit

Hampton Roads Publishing Company
publishes and distributes books on a variety of subjects,
including metaphysics, health, complementary medicine,
visionary fiction, and other related topics.

To receive a copy of our latest catalog, call toll-free,
(800) 766-8009, or send your name and address to:

Hampton Roads Publishing Company, Inc.
134 Burgess Lane
Charlottesville, VA 22902